The **PANORAMIC** Image

The Panoramic Image

Published by the John Hansard Gallery
The University, Southampton, 1981

with financial assistance from E. Leitz (Instruments) Ltd. and Sotheby's

ISBN 0-85432-211-6

Filmset and printed in Great Britain by
BAS Printers Limited, Over Wallop, Hampshire

Contents

Foreword

The idea for an exhibition on the theme of 'The Panoramic Image' came about when discussions were taking place in 1978 to decide on an appropriate exhibition to mark the opening of the John Hansard Gallery, which has been formed by amalgamating the previously separate Photographic Gallery and Art Gallery at the University of Southampton.

The main emphasis of exhibitions in the Gallery will be on contemporary work, but as the Gallery is part of a University tradition it will also take note of the past and of other disciplines.

In the light of this, the theme of 'The Panoramic Image' seemed to offer an extremely suitable subject for an opening exhibition. It allowed various visual media to be presented; it was a phenomenon which had historical as well as contemporary applications; it could work at a number of different levels. In short, it encapsulated much of the essence of the new Gallery.

By its very nature the subject matter of 'The Panoramic Image' was difficult to handle physically and academically. However, it constituted an exciting challenge which was accepted. The resultant exhibition has brought together a large collection of work, but it should not be viewed in any way as an attempt to provide a definitive statement on the subject. It merely offers a starting point for further research and interest and indicates ways in which some artists and photographers have used the idea of the panorama during the past few hundred years.

The work in the exhibition is supplemented by essays written for the catalogue by individual members of the team commissioned by the Gallery to put together the exhibition. Dr. John Sweetman, Senior Lecturer in the History of Art and Fine Art at the University of Southampton dealt with the history of the panorama until mid-nineteenth century. Jonathan Bayer, an American photographer resident in London, researched the use of the panoramic concept in photography and Dr. Brandon Taylor, art historian and ex-principal of Winchester School of Art, explored how modern artists had experimented with the panoramic image.

All three contributors were noble in their efforts on behalf of the project. Special thanks are also due to Francis Pugh who came in at a critical late stage to co-ordinate the exhibition and under whose wise guidance it finally took shape. As far as the catalogue itself is concerned BAS Printers Ltd. and Eric Molden, the designer, took the project to heart and together with James Fraser of Zwemmer Ltd. ensured that the efforts of all concerned with the exhibition would be complemented expertly and sympathetically in print.

The most warming feature of the whole exercise, however, has been the extraordinary goodwill, generosity, patience and trust of many individuals and institutions who have lent work to a gallery which to most of them is entirely unknown. They are all listed elsewhere in the catalogue, but I should like to take this opportunity of expressing the deep gratitude of the Gallery for their help.

The Gallery is also greatly indebted to Richard Baronio, Mr. Harold Barkley and Mr. Lionel Lambourne (Victoria and Albert Museum), Mr. Ralph Hyde (Guildhall Library), Mr. Peyton Skipwith (Fine Art Society), Mr. John Hopkins (Society of Antiquaries), Mr. David Robinson, Mr. Brian Polden, Dr. William Vaughan, Dr. Helmut Börsch-Supan (Verwaltung der Staatlichen Schlösser und Gärten, Berlin) and Professor Paul Smith.

The evolution of the John Hansard Gallery was a considerable act of faith by the University of Southampton. It is to be hoped that 'The Panoramic Image' exhibition will justify the confidence shown in the concept of the Gallery by both the University and other benefactors.

Leo Stable

Introduction

'Painting is brush lines. . . . In adhering to its laws one unfolds all forms, and in wielding the brush one sweeps over thousands of miles'.
Han Cho, 'Collection of the Purity of Landscape', 1121 (tr. Goepper)
'So the wide World's vast Volume, here we see To Miniature reduc'd, and just Epitome'.
Anon., 'Verses occasioned by the Sight of a Chamera Obscura', London 1747

The first words have an unmistakably oriental ring; it is no surprise to find they were written in the twelfth century by a Chinese mystic. Out of context they might have been pinned to the wall by a number of the Western artists whose imagination was caught by the panoramic vision, and whose work features in this exhibition. A certain parallel can even be followed between a Chinese landscape handscroll, comprehensive in its sweep yet unwound and mentally explored bit by bit, and a Western panoramic painting or photograph, 'unfolding all forms' and taken in section by section. Both emphasize the horizontal dimension, the idea of continuity; there is in both a time element, a stress on process, on which Brandon Taylor, writing of the twentieth-century panorama, has interesting things to say in his essay which follows. There all resemblance ends. Looking at the Chinese scroll the observer, as he unrolls, becomes a participant, re-enacts the path marked out by the artist, is absorbed into the painting and the creative processes which brought it into being. Contemplating the Western panorama, sprung on him in one *coup d'oeil* of which he cannot but remain conscious as he explores, he is on his own.

Nevertheless the idea of access to the 'all-embracing view', which a panorama—as Brandon Taylor reminds us— by definition offers, could be used by Western artists to stimulate or beguile the observer in many different ways. This exhibition is concerned with the phenomenon of the panoramic vision in art over more than four hundred years. The three essays which follow consider this in different contexts, corresponding to the three sections of the exhibition. The first discusses developments in the three centuries before 1850. These developments were, in essence, the rise of the form of landscape art which conveyed, through horizontal 'prospects', both information and a sense of extended space; and the growth in the minds of painters and scenographers of the idea of public spectacles showing natural wonders and human epics, which eventually, from about 1800, enclosed the spectator in a full circle. In the second essay Brandon Taylor pursues the panoramic image after 1850 and especially the linking of concepts of space, time and change in twentieth-century versions of it; he then discusses in detail a number of contemporary artists who have extended the panoramic idea in various ways. Jonathan Bayer's essay concentrates on the enormous impact of the photograph in both aesthetic and technological terms on the panoramic image. The use of the panoramic camera for creative rather than for merely documentary purposes clearly initiated a new and crucial phase of awareness.

One idea connects the many sea-changes of the panorama and all the essays take note of it. This is the notion of a work of art which succeeds by diffusion rather than concentration of interest. It is a notion which is of peculiar concern in Western art, since it runs counter to the tidal pressures of the European classical tradition to which we are still sensitive. That tradition stressed, in the humanist and human figure-orientated forms of Renaissance art, the ideal of the enclosed object—be it picture, sculpture or building—which answered, in some degree, the human desire for concentrated order and the artist's wish for formal unity. Against this preoccupation real-life landscape stood apart. With its extended proliferation of forms, landscape represented, according to the particular artist's point of view, two things: a world to be restrained or regulated, or a world of release, affording lines of direction for the eye and imagination to explore freely. In practice the second view increasingly suffuses the first. For evidence that Leonardo found the direction-lines of open landscape infinitely suggestive to the imagination we have only to look at the background to the *Mona Lisa*: his notes on painting in fact make the point explicitly.

By the eighteenth century the sense of satisfaction that the world's 'vast Volume' is reducible to 'just Epitome' is balanced by the consolations of spreading 'prospects' in art which infuse the layout of real-life landscape parks. Even a pillar of classical doctrine like Gerard de Lairesse, the 'Dutch Poussin', in his *Art of Painting* (1707), writes of landscape using language in which direction-lines everywhere reinforce the idea of release: 'Because the Soul, as pent up in a Dungeon, calls for Enlargement . . . what is more acceptable than shady Groves, open Parks, clear Waters, Rocks, Fountains, high Mountains and deep misty Valleys? All these we can see at once; and how relieving must the sight be to the most melancholy

Temper.'

'All these we can see at once': in this context the mountain-top panorama in real life is clearly very special. It affords the free sweep of these direction-lines, overwhelmingly horizontal, within the limits of an apparent circle of which the observer is the central point. It is freely spatial and yet can also be anthropocentric with an intensity that no more episodic landscape can rival. Some commentators have noticed the power it gives the observer: Gombrich, in *Art and Illusion*, points out that a real-life panorama enables us to assign imaginary equal distances to remote objects inside the apparent circle of vision. Others have been more conscious of its self-sufficiency: Adrian Stokes, in *Greek Culture and the Ego*, sees it as a visual equivalent of concerted sound, made up of 'harmony within melody and warring voices, of bits and polarities as they become a whole that is self-sufficient'. Not that one has to be a student of illusion or perception to feel a response: in whatever way the observer reacts to the panoramic view, the fact that he *is* moved by it has the testimony of innumerable writers from Petrarch onwards.

If the stimulus of the real-life panorama can be traced so vividly in the case of writers, what indeed of artists, to whom its visual qualities might be expected to communicate an added force? Three groups of artists require mention here. At the furthest remove from sympathy with panoramic art are the European art academies, working towards ideals of figure and history painting, officially awarding landscape a lowly status. Even so Reynolds, the Royal Academy's first President, encourages, as we shall see, the first full-circle panorama painting. In a middle group we find artists interested in investigating distance in relation to foreground figures, among these painters Leonardo, and Stubbs with his classically-judged friezes of foreground horses in front of open horizons. To this kind of artist the relation of the horizontal in landscape to the horizontal as the fundamental dimension of classical art is evidently of great importance. Alongside this group come the out-and-out pursuers of distance in the form of topographical views surveyed from hill-top or roof-top. From Dürer and Breughel the line runs forward to the 1800s, the era of specialised exhibition buildings and, above all, the Romantic imagination, which liberates the full spatial experience in painting.

In the nineteenth century public panoramas of landscape and history subjects—genres improbably but successfully linked on equal terms at last—hold sway in the cities and towns of the Western world. Free by virtue of their very excesses from the confusions which beset the more conventional categories of painting in the academies, they flourish and entertain, like the *Victoria regia* lily, in their purpose-built structures. Free also of the controversy that accompanies the new movements in art and, as Brandon Taylor points out, of the obligation to be avant-garde, the artist's panorama passes into the twentieth century.

In this century, less ostentatiously than in the last, but with impressive persistence and recharged inventiveness, the panoramic image has been demonstrating its ancient powers of attraction in many areas of painting and photography. More immediately accessible than much contemporary art, and stirring the memory of every one of us who has experienced the real-life effect, the artist's panorama continues to throw strong light on the needs, hankerings and enjoyments of successive generations.

The Japanese artist Hiroshige has a woodblock design of a hawk in close-up stooping over a panoramic landscape, the 10,000-acre plain at Suzaki. No Western artist seems to have produced a counterpart of such elemental force. But as a constant of Western art in many countries in the last four centuries the panorama deserves considerably greater recognition. Like the map of Africa in the not-so-distant past, much detail remains to be filled in.

John Sweetman

The Panoramic Image
The Period to 1850

'Panorama painting seems all the rage'
John Constable,
letter to J. Dunthorne,
26th May 1803.

We should not expect Constable, with his depth of feeling for a square mile or so of Suffolk and every intimate detail of life within it, to be moved by the full-circle public panoramas of his day, and on the whole he was not. But his words point to the delight and astonishment which they were then evoking in many who went to them. The young Ruskin was among these, and so was Wordsworth who wrote about his experience in Book VII of *The Prelude*. The physical scale of these panoramic paintings would have ruled out all possibility of showing any in this exhibition: it is in any case a peculiar problem of the subject that nothing survives of the pioneering English ones made between 1790 and 1830.[1] Enough remains of more portable material, however, to prove the

1 Baldassare Peruzzi, Sala delle Prospettive, Farnesina, Rome, *c.* 1516

fascination for artists and public of a form of production which attempted to fuse a number of surprisingly disparate ingredients: theatrical event and fine art painting, ephemeral amusement and edifying or instructional message, matter-of-fact topicality and imaginative stimulus. How it did this is a subject which until recently has received little attention; any investigator in the field must now acknowledge indebtedness to Richard Altick's copiously-documented treatment of the panorama as a social phenomenon in his book *The Shows of London* (1978).

The object of the present essay is to discuss the background of the panorama in art up to 1850. It is proposed to do this under two heads: first, the artist's pursuit of illusion, with its corollary, the spectator's suspension of disbelief; and secondly the human desire for information presented in the most understandable form. To some extent the two are inseparable. As the spectator viewed an all-encompassing nineteenth-century panorama painting both were involved in his experience and helped to account for his pleasure. It will be useful, however, to try to separate them. By so doing we shall better be able to judge the cumulative effect of such a painting, and evaluate the particular role and artistic worth of the panorama in that crucial century.

The pursuit of illusion in both Western and Eastern art is recorded in numerous anecdotes from ancient times. Two of the basic considerations of the classical tradition in Europe were the regard for art as the imitation of nature and the premium placed on skill in producing the imitation. The pursuit of exact imitation ran counter to the Aristotelian theory which recommended artists to use imitation to improve on natural appearances and arrive at ideals of visual beauty. Nevertheless it has a firm place in artistic theory and practice: the Roman writer Pliny's story about the Greek artist Zeuxis (*c.* 400 B.C.) who painted grapes which the sparrows pecked at, only to be worsted himself when he attempted to pull back a painted curtain in the studio of his friend Parrhasios, set a model for centuries to come.[2]

Interest in simulating natural appearances exactly could sometimes extend to whole settings with painted architecture. The theatre was an obvious influence here and Pliny describes painted stage scenery on which crows tended to alight.[3] A room which gave the illusion of a papyrus grove with birds sitting on its fronds existed at El Amarneh, Egypt, as early as about 1370 B.C.

The tenacity of the imitative as distinct from the idealising tendency in classical art has been well documented in recent years, notably by Ernst Kris and Otto Kurz.[4] They show how belief in the ability of mythical artist-figures like Daedalus the sculptor and Hephaestus the craftsman-god to endow their creations with life and motion leads to a view of the artist as one who both bestows life and creates substitutes for the real world. The many anecdotes of the Zeuxis-Parrhasios type indicate the strength in man's nature of the idea of identifying the picture with the thing depicted. Kris and Kurz present evidence supporting the view that whereas in primitive societies (and in children) objects are directly endowed with magical meaning which may have little to do with representation (a child's stick becomes a hobby-horse), in more evolved societies esteem for representation increases and naturalism takes on a special significance, answering the need for having the gap closed between the picture and what is depicted.

Part of the impact afforded by the illusionistic panorama painting is clearly explicable in terms of this kind of analysis. But it is noticeable that response to the deceptive power of painted illusion is not the preserve of the connoisseur: it is shared with the layman and, as the author of the Zeuxis story would have us believe, with birds and animals. Henry Aston Barker, one of the most prominent and gifted initiators of the early nineteenth-century panorama, recalled that when he and his father hung their painting of the grand fleet at Spithead at the Leicester Square rotunda in 1794 and the Royal Family viewed it, the Queen felt seasick.[5] At the same show a Newfoundland dog is said to have leapt from the viewing platform to join painted capsized sailors in the painted sea. Both criteria of success in the Zeuxis-type story were satisfied: the illusion deceived not only the human eye but that of the animal also.

The panorama painting of this type clearly aimed to push *trompe l'oeil* to its ultimate by encircling the spectator with illusion. In the cool light of dawn, Barker, however

2 Paul Sandby, Room from Drakelowe Hall, Derbyshire, 1793

(shrewd performer as he was), would have agreed that if the reactions of the Queen and the dog were in the manner he described, it was for reasons other than the power of illusion. For it was patently obvious that painted panoramas with immobile figures in them could never achieve full illusion: the capsized sailors would never drown neither would they scramble to safety. Landscape panoramas without figures stood a better chance of total illusionistic success—but water was always a problem and so was any attempt to simulate the movement of the sun.

Yet still the panoramas drew the crowds. Many reasons led to their success and effect on visitors and some of these reasons will be examined later. One surely had to do with what people knew of the conventions of 'normal' pictures and the expectations they brought into the panorama building with them. One expectation was sustained by the 'human-interest' panorama which, for a season and on a grand scale, perpetuated a moment of spectacle, no doubt to the satisfaction of the overwhelming majority of visitors. But another expectation was not sustained: the panorama made it necessary to move one's head and assimilate a vast, indeed often continuous, area of canvas which defied the logic of any conventional painting with

an easily-grasped focal centre of attention. The experience of feelings akin to seasickness in a proportion of visitors in such circumstances would not perhaps be surprising.

Whatever problems of illusionism the painter of public panoramas felt he could never solve satisfactorily, he had one immense advantage over the public and rival artists—he could control utterly certain viewing conditions under which his work was seen (except on dark days or at night). Renaissance artists had much discussed the question of relating pictorial effects and especially painted perspectives to the point of view of the spectator. The drawback to most of these effects was that they worked from only one position in front of the picture, far less well if the spectator moved to one side or another or forwards to examine detail.[6] The panorama painter could at least restrict the movement of his spectator to a fairly tight viewing platform placed at the right distance from the picture surface. In such conditions, if the spectator could not 'get at' the painting, the painting could 'get at' him, and clearly often did.

We are used to thinking of Renaissance art as anthropocentric and inclined to naturalism. It is true that the greatest Italian artists of the period placed special emphasis on the ideal and played down (without ignoring) *trompe l'oeil*. But it could also be said that in so far as natural appearances were adapted to the spectator's expectations the conditions for an art of more generous illusion were being prepared. A notable step towards illusion was to paint a naturalistic view and frame it by painted architecture which appeared to continue the spectator's own space, as Peruzzi, a pupil of Raphael, did with his panoramic view of Rome in the Farnesina about 1516 (Illustration 1). Half a century later a visitor to Palladio's Villa Maser could get caught up in Veronese's landscape murals which cleverly continue on their painted surfaces the lines of the actual landscape seen from the windows, and immerse himself in the beautifully-judged *trompe l'oeil* of painted figures standing in painted doorways. The stage was being set for the full-blown exploitation of illusion in combination with the arts of theatre scenography in the painting of the seventeenth-century Baroque. Tassi's saloon at the Palazzo Lancellotti in Rome, with a seaport seen through painted openings

3 Aelbert Cuyp, *Dordrecht from the Maas, c.* 1660

beyond opulent painted architecture, was begun in 1617. A similar theme occurs in the earliest surviving Panorama Room in England, at Eastbury, Essex, done at the same period.[7]

The final step was to leave out the architectural frame altogether and open the interior to nature, as Cipriani was perhaps the first whole-heartedly to do in the parlour at Standlynch (later Trafalgar House, Wilts.) about 1766. This has a continuous painted landscape round the flat walls: nine years later Sir George Beaumont appears to have been considering embellishing his house with a *circular* landscape room which was unfortunately not carried out. The Drakelowe Hall interior of 1793 (Illustration 2) by Paul Sandby, preserved at the Victoria and Albert Museum, also presented a continuous landscape and instead of painted classical architecture has real palings with wicket gates lined up near the walls, an effect greeted a year later by Anna Seward, who was tempted to

enter the painted forest glades: 'a landscape deception', she wrote, 'little inferior to the watery delusion of the celebrated panorama.'[8]

Anna Seward's musings alert us again to the importance of a sensitive observer's willingness to go along with a pictorial illusion. Part of the success of the nineteenth-century panoramas was surely the result of a frank surrender to virtuosity, that spell-binding capacity of an artist who, through absolute control of his medium, disarms informed criticism and overrides lay disbelief. Virtuosity in art had been highlighted in the modern world by Vasari when he related how Giotto had drawn a perfect circle freehand. That the process of transforming a challenge into an immaculate triumph has a deep-running appeal to the human mind is shown by the many versions of this story which is also recounted of Dürer and, in the Chinese tradition, of the eighth-century artist Wu Tao-tzu.

Virtuosity makes difficulty seem easy, calculation spontaneous and ingenuity an end in itself. Illusion and the cult of the showpiece go hand in hand with it, and by the seventeenth century operated on many levels, from the scenic transformations of court masques to the fairground and tavern spectacles at which gentlemen mingled with artisans to see the latest marvels.[9] And if the eye was willing to be led, there were devices ready to lead it, in this age of optical experiment. Among these we must note the camera obscura or 'dark-room'. This took many forms but was essentially a box fitted with lens and mirror which cast an image onto a flat surface: the head could often be put right inside it. It had its uses for topographical artists, but carried aesthetic experience in its own right: Addison was delighted by one at Greenwich Park in 1712 which gave him 'the Picture of a Ship entering at one end, and sailing by Degrees through the whole Piece'[10]. We may detect here that satisfaction with continuous movement in the horizontal plane, which was to be a strong ploy in the big marine panorama presentations of a century later.

An eighteenth-century minor obsession with shows involving movement—lighted peepshows, shadow-plays, tragedies performed by lifesize wax marionettes—prepared the ground for Loutherbourg's famous Eidophusikon of 1781, a show which combined form, colour, movement and sound with an unprecedented skill resulting from its creator's long experience of stagecraft. Burke's exposition of the Sublime and its terrors had appeared over twenty years earlier. At the Eidophusikon 'sublime' subjects as diverse as Niagara and Milton's Pandemonium were brilliantly recreated. The Eidophusikon's stage was only ten feet wide, but its ambitious scope and powerful projection of effects made for a physical magnitude of presentation which undoubtedly prefigured the panorama as a staged spectacle.[11]

While the showmanship of the late eighteenth century certainly aimed to stimulate its audiences imaginatively with evocations of the sublime or of travel to faraway places, it must also be recognized that much of it was concerned with the presentation of fact. The Eidophusikon's first season showed a sequence called 'Moonlight, a View in the Mediterranean, the Rising of the Moon contrasted with the effect of Fire', which reminds us of the acuity of observation, both soberly truthful and romantically evocative, being brought simultaneously to such effects of light by the painter Wright of Derby. A combination of the sense of marvel with the analysis of the contemporary world—seen also in the writings of contemporary Erasmus Darwin—had been brilliantly caught by Wright in his famous picture An Experiment with an Airpump (1768) in which an 'expert' natural philosopher demonstrates in a darkened interior to an audience of laymen. Such an attitude also contributes a strand leading to the great age of the large-scale panorama after 1800.

We have already reached our second heading—the human desire for factual information. This closely connects the early topographical drawings in this exhibition with nineteenth-century panoramic examples such as David Roberts' View of Cairo (Illustration 27),

which was actually used for a public panorama. The development of the topographical drawing in Europe, half plan, half bird's-eye view, was itself intimately linked with the work of map-makers and land-surveyors. Already in the sixteenth century drawings, woodcuts and engravings of towns and military encampments were being done which included large sweeps of countryside, and Dürer's Siege of a Fortress (1527, Illustration 23) shows a parallel development in regard to scenes of actual warfare. A genre of long drawings, of 'prospects', which authentically recorded buildings, became established: before 1550 Anton van der Wyngaerde had produced one of London, Westminster and Southwark that was ten feet long and seventeen inches high. The panoramic vision was powerfully fed by such works.[12] Dürer's inclusion in his 1527 print of a foreground ridge, between the spectator and the view, is an abrupt example of a device which a Baroque artist like Hollar later converts into a dynamically curving slope on which the spectator is invited to stand (see Tangier from the Land).

In the 1660s and 70s, the Bohemian artist Wenceslaus Hollar vigorously unites in England the roles of map-maker, panoramist and 'scenographer' to Charles II. In his Tangier series (cat no. 2) he gives us a single subject from a variety of viewpoints on land and at sea. Not unexpectedly the presence of water could attract the panoramist down from the heights, real or imaginary, to the coast or riverbank. In Holland in the same years Cuyp was giving subtlety as well as sonority to the genre of townscape painting in such masterpieces as his Dordrecht from the Maas (Illustration 3) itself of panoramic shape.

Eighteenth-century travel gave topographical art fresh encouragements. First came the heyday of the Grand Tour of Italy and the commissioning of view-paintings as momentoes. Working in Venice and England Canaletto, at mid-century, combined in his panoramic subjects a dramatic elegance of line with an extraordinary ability to project the feeling of air. This spaciousness and clarity are conspicuous in his two great views of London from Richmond House (c. 1747, Illustration 4). Secondly geographical exploration was developing contacts well beyond Europe. The establishment of British rule in Bengal in the 1770s and 80s produced a spate of Indian views by artists.

In the years up to the establishment of Thomas Cook's conducted tours in the 1830s and beyond, such records of distant places were collected not only by those who had travelled but by those who stayed at home. Country after country came into fashionable focus. Of perennial interest for panoramists was the skyline of Constantinople. With Islamic lands attracting more and more attention, publications such as Denon's book on Egypt of 1802 (following Napoleon's expedition of 1798), drew increasing numbers of artists and other visitors to Cairo (Illustration 27)[13].

Over the same years, the spread of newspapers (unillustrated) stimulated an interest in current events and visual renderings of them. Benjamin West's Death of Wolfe of 1770–1 had depicted a modern subject, and was followed by paintings of other contemporary scenes which frequently assumed large size (Copley's Defeat of the Floating Batteries of 1786–91 was 18 by 25 feet). The cult of 'gigantism', which Boase noted[14], flourished in the years of the French Revolution and Napoleon. It was in fact a symptom of the age of exhibitions, and the display in isolation by such major figures as West, Copley and Jacques Louis David of single pictures which could attract multitudes and earn large sums through engraved editions was a development which unquestionably favoured public panoramas.[15] The size of these large paintings could nevertheless make them hard to show. John Thomas Smith saw James Ward's enormous Triumph of Wellington of 1816 (22 by 35 feet) at Chelsea Hospital not only suspended without a frame (just as a fairground showman, he said, would put out a large canvas to display the portraits of 'a giant, the Pig-faced Lady, or the Fire-Eater') but with its lower part projecting over a gallery 'just like the lid of a kitchen salt-box'.[16]

Professionally-planned panoramic displays, however, were to afford answers to many of these difficulties, providing the would-be traveller and the news-hungry with vivid experiences of places and events famous in history and the contemporary scene, and doing it in purpose-made buildings and in ideal conditions.

The first true panorama painting that extended round a full circle appears to have been done by Robert Barker (1739–1806) of Edinburgh. Sitting on top of Calton Hill in

1786–7, he rotated a square frame around 360 degrees and made drawings forming a continuous prospect. With the help of his son Henry Aston Barker (1774–1856) he went on to draw up plans for putting such views on show, and in 1789 transferred the idea with Sir Joshua Reynolds's blessing to London. He called his show 'la Nature à Coup d'Oeil', but a friend dubbed it 'Panorama' in 1791. Barker opened at the Leicester Square rotunda in 1794. Two subjects, painted in oils, were on view, a smaller one of 50 feet diameter above a larger one of 90 feet (283 feet round). Both were lit solely by windows in the roof (out of sight) and were viewed from central platforms. The lower of these platforms was approached from below, the upper from outside stairs, so that no door interrupted the lateral flow of the panoramic images. Deprived thus of all points of reference except those in the painting thirty feet away (about half the distance in the upper panorama), the spectator felt himself to be part of the painted event. C. R. Leslie remarked, after seeing Barker's Lisbon in 1812, 'the objects appear so real, that it is impossible to imagine at what distance the canvas is from the eye'.[17]

The panorama was to spread to the provinces, and numerous rivals to Leicester Square arose in London. In 1800 the great room of the Lyceum, Strand, showed Robert Ker Porter's *Taking of Seringapatam*—a painting over 200 feet long extending through half a circle. The work was acclaimed by Benjamin West, Reynolds's successor as President of the Royal Academy, who made the link with history painting: 'A WONDER OF THE WORLD . . . admirably done as it could have been by the best historical painter amongst us. . . .'[18] The Lyceum also staged, in 1802, Thomas Girtin's *Eidometropolis or Panorama of London* (from the southern end of Blackfriars Bridge, 18 by 108 feet), surely the most tantalizing loss to us from this period.[19] The sensitive drawings by Girtin's friend Henry Aston Barker of the same year for a panorama of Paris (Illustration 25) give inklings of a worthy rival.

The panorama idea was taking hold simultaneously in many other countries. William Winstanley showed a panorama of London in New York in 1795; The German Adam Breysig put on Rome in Berlin in 1800. Other

4 Antonio Canal, called Canaletto, *View of the Thames from Richmond House*, c. 1747

centres included Paris; St. Petersburg; and Salzburg, where the Sattler family were active in the second quarter of the new century. In New York John Vanderlyn recreated Versailles in a panorama of 1817 painted on three thousand square feet of canvas.

After the Napoleonic Wars panoramic shows and publications blossomed. In 1822 there opened near the Place de la République, Paris, the Diorama of Louis Jacques Mandé Daguerre, the future pioneer of photography. The painted Diorama was flat, but partly translucent, allowing illumination from both sides; its appearance was therefore continually being transformed by changes of lighting. It opened in the following year in Regent's Park, London. The Diorama was to have special appeal to seated audiences, through its emphasis on movement and sequences of visual experience, and itself was much copied, especially in theatres where (after 1817) gas light was used on stage. 'Serious' artists like Clarkson Stanfield and David Roberts did many designs for such entertainments.[20] Panoramic views moving across the stage gave the audience, for instance, the illusion of sailing down the Rhine, or across Virginia Water. A handbill of Bartholomew Fair of 1831[21] reminds us of the educational role of dioramas: a reconstruction is offered of the recently-fought naval action at Navarino, with 'portraits' of the English vessels involved.

Such large-scale enactments had their portable counterparts. 'Journeys' in strip form, between towns and along rivers or coasts appeared in considerable numbers in the 1820s, a lively example being Havell's *Cruise along the Southern Coast of Kent* with its transition from stormy skies and choppy waters out at sea to tranquil conditions near harbour.

One of the most prominent places where Panoramas, Dioramas and 'Cosmoramas' could be seen was Vauxhall Gardens, the celebrated London entertainment centre. This had opened in 1732 and in its early days had made a feature of paintings as diverting incidents set up in its walks and alleys, some incorporating illusionistic extensions to these spaces. Subjects exhibited at Vauxhall after Waterloo included sunsets and moonlights, marines, Gothic abbeys, Venice from the Adriatic, Captain Ross's Expedition to the North Pole, and that gift of 1834 to the

panorama industry, the Burning of the Houses of Parliament.

Meanwhile, the Barkers' efforts at Leicester Square were continued by their associates and eventual successors, John and Robert Burford. The Leicester Square panoramas endured till 1863. We are left with a still-emotive memorial of their variousness in the form of the descriptive sixpenny booklets which were available at the door, reproducing the panorama of the day in outline and giving a summary of the facts about the scene or event depicted (cat. no. 23).

Perhaps the most extraordinary of all the static panoramas opened in 1829 in the newly-built Colosseum, Regent's Park. (Illustration 27) showing a view of London as seen from the top of St. Paul's. This work was first imagined by Thomas Hornor, a surveyor who, through the summer of 1821, made detailed drawings from a cabin perilously poised above the cross on the top of the Cathedral[22]. As carried out by Edmund Thomas Parris, the painting filled the rotunda and gave an illusion of the capital stretching in every direction for twenty miles to Windsor Castle, Epping Forest and Greenwich (Illustration 28). Ironically, the very permanence of this gigantic work, covering 46,000 square feet of canvas, contributed to the decline of the Colosseum's fortunes: the view of London was speedily outdated—the Colosseum itself, a post-1821 building, never appeared—and the essence of panoramas at this date was accuracy. Despite many novelties staged there, the building was forced to close in 1863, the fateful year also for Leicester Square. At the height of its reputation, however, the painting crystallized the panoramic effect in all its plenitude. Standing on one of the viewing platforms, the spectator beheld, to magnificent effect, the Thames looping through the City towards an ideally-clear, unbroken horizon, beneath a luminous sky spread around and above it. How one wonders what Turner thought of it.

How one would also like to know, for that matter, what that remarkable painter John Martin thought of the Colosseum panorama. His recreations of cityscapes such as ancient Babylon, with rows of columns leading into huge and heady distances, owed much to Turner, to Milton's description of the Palace of Pandemonium, and

5 Caspar David Friedrich, *The Monk by the Sea*, 1809

perhaps to Schinkel's architecture and other sources.[23] Beginning in 1816, the first of the series also antedate Parris's painting. But it is worth recalling that Martin published explanatory pamphlets with 'keys' in the manner of the panoramic shows. The Martinesque painter Francis Danby made a model of the diorama in 1827 and no doubt saw Marshall's travelling panoramas in Bristol[24]. Thomas Cole reflected a true panoramic concept in his painting *The Architect's Dream* (1840), done in America. From the top of a column the visionary architect surveys a spread of buildings in a mixture of architectural styles, a conceit palpably assisted by the public city-panoramas[25].

So we return to the matter of the indisputable power, as illusion, of these all- or part-encompassing works, to face unavoidable questions. Were they also art? How did they relate to 'serious' painting? In the absence of a range of early extant examples, we can merely use as clues the words of such contemporaries as Benjamin West, already quoted. A more artful question may allow us to go a little further. If there is agreement that the greatest works of art all convey an over-arching unity of form, shape or climax, does this place the panorama painting—by definition the most diffused of all paintings—at the opposite end of the scale of value? Here we can surely say no. The period 1800–1850 was one of radically-changing attitudes in the visual arts. By 1800 classicism was losing ground to two near-contemporary pictures which are panoramic in their implications if not in their proportions: Friedrich's *The Monk by the Sea* (1809, Illustration 5) and Turner's *Snow Storm—Hannibal crossing the Alps* (1812).

It took the Romantics to discover the remoteness of the sea as a source of the panoramic experience. The alien qualities which had previously deflected even Breughel from this now took on an ineluctable attraction. Friedrich's work setting a tiny figure against an expanse of ocean transforms the sea-painting into something poignant and personal[26]. Turner's *Hannibal*, we know, gestated in his mind for over two years following the experience of a severe storm in Yorkshire. Thirty years later he produced a successor, the *Snow Storm—Steam Boat off a Harbour's Mouth* (1842, Illustration 6). Turner vigorously maintained the truth of the story that he had lived through this storm lashed to the mast of a ship at sea[27]. Such a situation—the central point, the surrounding vortex—might at first sight seem to make Turner the arch-panoramist of all time. But if his insistence on the central experience was shared with the Victorian panorama-painter, the manner in which he expressed it was radically different. The degree of subjectivity of Turner's treatment was as far from the effect of a public panorama as this was from the coolly-intellectual experience of a rotunda by Palladio. Turner asserted that he did not paint the work to be understood: the panorama-painter had understanding as his over-riding purpose.

There was nevertheless more to the panorama-painter's work than this. Granted that the intent of the large-scale panorama was to make things effortless for the spectator, the great successes must surely have depended on powers of intellectual organization (as well as physical stamina) on the part of the artist that were of an uncommon order. There are indications of artists' successes that were not always public successes. Edward Edwards says that Girtin's *Eidometropolis* 'was not much noticed by the public'[28], and the *New Monthly Magazine* described it as 'the Connoisseur's panorama'. Nor perhaps has it been sufficiently appreciated how panorama organization from a roof-top did require careful selection to make the best of composition. We may have a

6 Joseph Mallord William Turner, *Snow Storm: Steam-boat off a Harbour's Mouth*, 1842

the Romantics, with their stress on subjective experience. The notion of a work of art as self-contained in its own world was still alive for the neo-classical architects who admired Paestum and Karnak. The growing concern with the ragged Gothic of Strasbourg and Tintern, however, was declaring an increasing regard for effects of space, void and changing light: if in architecture, how much

more so in painting, and if in landscape painting of conventional form, how much more so in that of panoramas. The changing light over the Bavarian Alps in the drawing by Sir George Scharf (1846, Illustration 29) provides an example.

The full impact of this Romantic attitude, taken to opposite extremes of stillness and turmoil, can be seen in glimpse of the high quality of the best performances when we note how in Henry Aston Barker's *Paris* sequence (Illustration 24) the great dome of the Invalides (the only major break on the horizon) is visually supported at the base of the drawing by the simple mass of the foreground house (the only building which rises from the baseline). It can be no coincidence that these two buildings assist each other in this way. Elemental use of the verticals of foreground buildings had been made for centuries by panoramists looking steeply down on them from their strange roof-top and hill-top world, as we see when we look from the Barker to Hollar's marvellous *Tangier* drawing (Illustration 23) with its upward-jutting lines of the fortification immediately below the gentle summit of the laterally-flowing hills.

In the twentieth century, when so much of the best painting has been austere or private or both, or has been presented in terms of guru-like cult figures, it is easy to dismiss the Victorian public panorama as trivializing in both intention and content. Ruskin can correct us here. We have his important if tantalizingly brief testimony concerning an 'exquisitely painted' panorama of Milan from the roof of the Cathedral that he saw as a boy of fourteen at Leicester Square[29]. Ruskin's admiration of the panorama seen from a high point may perhaps be set in relation to his admiration of mountains seen from the plain, as providing revelations of the multiplicity he loved ('tree after tree . . . in successive height, one behind another . . .') and what he calls the 'power of redundance'.[30] To us redundance signifies merely excess. Ruskin valued it as prodigality. Perhaps we should reflect on that. In that light the panorama painting of Ruskin's youth was a vehement purveyor of redundance, but a redundance that was calculated and explicit. And though by 1850 it had little left to say in its show-business context, the concept—as the other sections of this exhibition prove—was far from dead.

John Sweetman

Notes

(Books published London unless otherwise stated)

(1) Existing examples of the old-style public panorama are relatively scarce. They survive at The Hague (Panorama Mesdag), Innsbruck, Lucerne, Budapest, Moscow, in the United States (including one in store at the Metropolitan Museum of Art, New York), and London (Victoria and Albert Museum).

(2) Pliny, *Natural History*, 35: p. 65. For interesting comment on the story see E. H. Gombrich, *Art and Illusion*, 5th ed. 1977, p. 173.

(3) Pliny, *ibid.*, 35: p. 23.

(4) E. Kris and O. Kurz, *Legend, Myth and Magic in the Image of the Artist*, New Haven and London, 1979, p. 66. (originally *Die Legende vom Künstler*, Vienna 1934). *See also* Gombrich, *op cit.*, *passim*. Useful comparative material from the Far Eastern traditions is found in R. Goepper, *The Essence of Chinese Painting*, 1963, p. 24.

(5) R. Altick, *The Shows of London*, Cambridge, Mass. and London 1978, p. 189.

(6) J. White, *The Birth and Rebirth of Pictorial Space*, 1967 (ed. 1972), p. 194.

(7) For a full list of panoramic rooms in Britain see E. Croft-Murray, *Decorative Painting in England*, II, 1970, p. 306.

(8) Letter to the Rev. T. S. Whalley, 25th July 1794, quoted Croft-Murray, *op. cit.*, p. 62.

(9) For details of these last see Altick, *op. cit.*, pp. 7, 34.

(10) *Spectator*, 25th June 1712.

(11) In 1779 Loutherbourg had devised, with R. B. Sheridan, a pantomime 'The Wonders of Derbyshire', which is of some interest as, for the first time on the British stage, the landscape settings were the *raison d'être* of the action, which was merely an excuse for changing the scenery. See Rudiger Joppien: *Philippe Jacques de Loutherbourg, RA, 1740–1812*, catalogue of exhibition at Kenwood House, London (Greater London Council) 1973.

(12) As regards Britain, the map-maker Christopher Saxton published his atlas in 1579. The *Particular Description of England* (1588) by William Smith (British Library, Sloane MS 2596) contains a fine drawing of London which is both bird's-eye view and skyline panorama. The 'country house view' became a popular vehicle for the bird's-eye view convention: for Britain, see also John Harris, *The Artist and the Country House, a history of country house and garden view painting in Britain 1540–1870*, 1979, and H. V. S. and M. S. Ogden, *English Taste in Landscape in the Seventeenth Century*, Ann Arbor 1955.

(13) Further discussion of Islamic themes in relation to public panoramas is contained in the present writer's forthcoming book *Islamic Inspiration in British and American Art*.

(14) T. S. R. Boase, *English Art 1800–1870*, 1959, p. 21.

(15) 'Fine Art' paintings and panoramas could find themselves in rivalry, as in Dublin in 1821, when Géricault's *Raft of the Medusa* was there on tour, and Messrs Marshall simultaneously ran a panorama of the same subject (*Saunders' Newsletter*, 17th February 1821 etc). See Lee Johnson, 'The Raft of the Medusa in Great Britain', *Burlington Magazine*, 96, 1954, p. 249.

(16) J. T. Smith, *A Book for a Rainy Day*, 1845, p. 278.

(17) C. R. Leslie, *Autobiographical Recollections*, ed. Tom Taylor, Boston 1860, p. 174.

(18) For full account see Altick, *op. cit.*, p. 135. The original source is Jane Porter (the artist's sister), in Thomas Frognall Dibdin. Reminiscences of a Literary Life, 1836, i, pp. 143–6.

(19) For the Eidometropolis see W. T. Whitley, 'Girtin's Panorama', *Connoisseur*, 69 (1924), pp. 13–20. Sketches survive in the British Museum.

(20) For much detail on Stanfield's panorama work see P. van der Merwe and R. Took, *Clarkson Stanfield 1793–1867*, exhibition catalogue. Tyne and Wear County Council Museums, 1979, p. 81.

(21) In Guildhall Library, London; reproduced Altick, *op. cit.*, fig. 62.

(22) Thomas Hornor (1785–1844) is a figure of great interest who illustrates the enduring nature of the links between land-surveyor and topographical artist, in his case leading straight to panoramas. A surveyor by training, he was describing himself in 1814 as 'Pictural Delineator of Estates', a year after producing a small book on his methods. His 1813 plan of Clerkenwell appears to include cloud shadows on the ground (see R. Hyde, 'Thomas Hornor: Pictural Land Surveyor', in *Imago Mundi*, 29, 1977, pp. 23–34.

(23) See W. Feaver, *The Art of John Martin*, 1975, p. 54. Martin's mezzotint (about 1825) of *Satan presiding over the Infernal Council*, with Satan, seated on a sphere, addressing multitudes concentrically arranged round him, is a striking panoramic image.

(24) See E. Adams, *Francis Danby: Varieties of Poetic Landscape*, 1973, p. 74.

(25) Reproduced in Feaver, *op. cit.*, pl. 80.

(26) In fact the Romantic consciousness of man's isolation in the face of nature's immensities ('I did not expect to escape', Turner said in his account of a snowstorm that he experienced at sea, see following note), was epitomised in specifically panoramic terms in a review of Friedrich's *The Monk by the Sea*, by the dramatist and poet Heinrich von Kleist, who saw the solitary monk looking out to sea as 'the sole spark of life in the vast realm of death, the lonely centre of a lonely circle' (quoted by R. Cardinal, *German Romantics in Context*, 1975, p. 71).

(27) Conversation with the Rev. William Kingsley, reported by Ruskin in the fifth ed. of his Notes on the Turners exhibited at Marlborough House. 1857. The story is quoted in full in M. Butlin and E. Joll, *The Paintings of J. M. W. Turner*, 1977, text vol., p. 224.

(28) E. Edwards, *Anecdotes of Painting*, 1808, p. 280. I am grateful to Francis Pugh for this reference. Edwards is writing about a showing of the work in the Great Room at Spring Gardens. See also L. Parris, *Landscape in Britain, c. 1750–1850*, Tate Gallery 1973, p. 115.

(29) Ruskin, *Praeterita*, in *Works*, ed. E. T. Cook and A. D. O. Wedderburn, 1902–12, xxxv, p. 117–8.

(30) Ruskin, *Modern Painters*, ch. xx. in *Works*, ed. cit., vi, p. 424.

The Panoramic Image: 1850 To The Present Day

'The earth expanding right hand and left hand . . .'
Walt Whitman, Leaves of Grass.

The idea of the panoramic image is an intriguing one. Artists have been devising visual panoramas of one sort or another since the beginnings of art. Yet its status as a 'type' is obscure. The panoramic image appears to have virtually no written history, and only a slender presence in conventional accounts of the development of art. The purpose of this exhibition is to rescue the panorama from relative neglect, and to do so by gathering together images from most periods of modern history and by standing them together as a group.

The fate of the panorama during the period from 1850 to the present, which is the concern of this section, is not an easy story to tell. Few recent or contemporary artists have consciously set out to produce panoramas, at least in the sense of Dr. Sweetman's essay. Yet clearly a large number of artists have shared enough attitudes with their eighteenth- and nineteenth-century forbears to make their work panoramic in effect. We shall see in due course what forms the contemporary versions have assumed. But for the essence of the concept we have to go much further back.

For me, Frederick Church's famous *Niagara Falls* of 1857 provides an excellent paradigm of the panoramic outlook (Illustration 7). Seven feet wide and three feet high, large and heroic in conception, it provides in visual terms an image of natural grandeur which is both optimistic and generous, and at the same time proprietorial in the best nineteenth-century manner. Church (1826–1900) marshalled all the resources of his art to provide what Tuckerman in his *Book of the Artists* (1867) calls 'the first satisfactory delineation by art of one of the greatest natural wonders of the western world.'[1] The painting is, of course, more than a 'satisfactory delineation'. It says in the strongest pictorial terms: I, Frederick Church, saw this natural vision, and here is my devotion. And the picture also signifies a kind of territorial victory, for by thus depicting the natural spectacle he had, at the same time, captured it. The Niagara Falls had similarly attracted the efforts of other American artists: Kensett, Vanderlyn, Cropsay, Trumbull, Bierstadt, and Innes, to name but a few, had all been drawn to it. Why? Partly from a sense of fashion, and partly because of the excitingly raw, undiscovered flavour of this extraordinary natural phenomenon—no doubt these factors played their part. But Church's image in particular, with its widescreen format and glowing colours, expressed something in the new American consciousness which by mid-century was becoming archetypal: particularly an appreciation of the spaciousness of the landscape and an upsurge of naive optimism which characterized the beginnings of American capitalism.

But it was two generations before Church's painting, and in a different part of the hemisphere, that a panorama actually so-called had been summoned into life for the first time. The word 'panorama' conjoins the Greek παν, meaning 'all', with οραμα, meaning 'view': the conjunction literally means something like 'all-embracing view' or 'entire view'. It was in eighteenth century Scotland that this usage was devised and given application to painting by a (then) little-known Edinburgh artist, Robert Barker, who in the spring of 1787 contrived a 360 degree wrap-around watercolour view of that city from the observatory on Calton Hill. For showing it he had applied for, and received, a patent for 'an entire new

7 F. Church, *Niagara Falls*, 1857

Contrivance or Apparatus, called La Nature à Coup d'Oeil, for the purpose of displaying Views of Nature at Large, by Oil Painting, Fresco, Watercolour, Crayons, or any other mode of Painting or Drawing.[2] Two years later, Barker exhibited his contraption at Number 28, The Haymarket, London, and the term 'panorama' was in public as well as private use. A mixture of topographical art, trompe l'oeil painting, and showbusiness, this early panorama by Barker was the first of a long line of public spectacles that populated Regency and early Victorian London. The Encyclopaedia Britannica of 1801 put the matter very fairly when it described 'panorama' as 'a word employed of late to denote a painting . . . which represents an entire view of an entire country, city or other natural objects, as they appear to a person standing in any situation and turning right round.'

By one of those inexplicable historical coincidences the idea of representing the full circle of the horizon on a circular canvas to give an illusion of being actually before the scene was arrived at almost simultaneously by the American artist William Dunlap (1766–1839) and by the German Adam Breysig (1766–1831). Dunlap recalls a conversation in the winter of 1784–5, with 'an English gentleman', in which he—Dunlap—had remarked to the gentleman that when he was a child he had had the idea of making a picture 'which should represent all surrounding objects as they appear in nature when we turn and look from a central spot', but that he had never spoken of it. 'Often, when standing on a eminence, and looking around me on the bright and glorious objects, here a landscape, there a bay and shipping—a city glittering in light—all the tints of a sky from the setting sun to the sober colours of the opposite horizon—I have imagined myself surrounded by an upright circular canvas, and depicting the scene just as nature displayed it . . .'. The Englishman then told Dunlap about Barker's experiments in Edinburgh. 'This was the first time I ever heard of a panorama' Dunlap exclaims, 'a species of picture then unknown to the world'.[3]

Barker's panorama, which was designed to be housed in a special building with light admitted only from certain directions and with devices included to prevent the observer from seeing above or below the painting, was intended from the outset to be part of mass entertainment. And indeed its commercial possibilities were revived, once the nineteenth-century panorama had disappeared, in the motion-picture industry of the twentieth century, with the use of the wide screen, and, more recently, with manneristic developments such as 'sensurround' in which smells and 3-D effects are projected out into the audience. The total, literally all-embracing hologram environment is perhaps only a few years away.

But between and beyond the big-business uses of visual panoramas (one could also mention the planetarium here) there is another story to tell, a story of image-making rather than of image-use. On close inspection one can see that the long horizontal image has formed a discernible—even if minor—thread in the fabric of modern art. Because for all the ingenious machinery which was invented to give it substance in the last century, the word 'panorama', as its Greek etymology suggests, really applies to the image *type* and not to the manner of its exhibition or its shape—and still less to its capacity for inflicting damage on the nervous system.

Moreover I think its main characteristics have always been more or less stable; it has always served documentary, information-gathering purposes, however subject these may be to individualistic control. And it has always done this at a certain distance from the subject, using an extra-wide horizontal format to convey a wide sweep of events, natural or otherwise. Thus there must be a certain objectivity of treatment; and depicted space. The painted panorama is, of course, a major instrument of landscape art.

We saw all these features (and more) in the early panorama by Church. And with the benefit of hindsight we can see that it was never essential to the panorama, even to Barker's, that it be housed in a circular contraption with hidden passageways and concealed light sources. The early topographical panoramas of the sixteenth century kept to the conventional rule that only

8 William Frith, *Life at the Seaside*, 1852–4

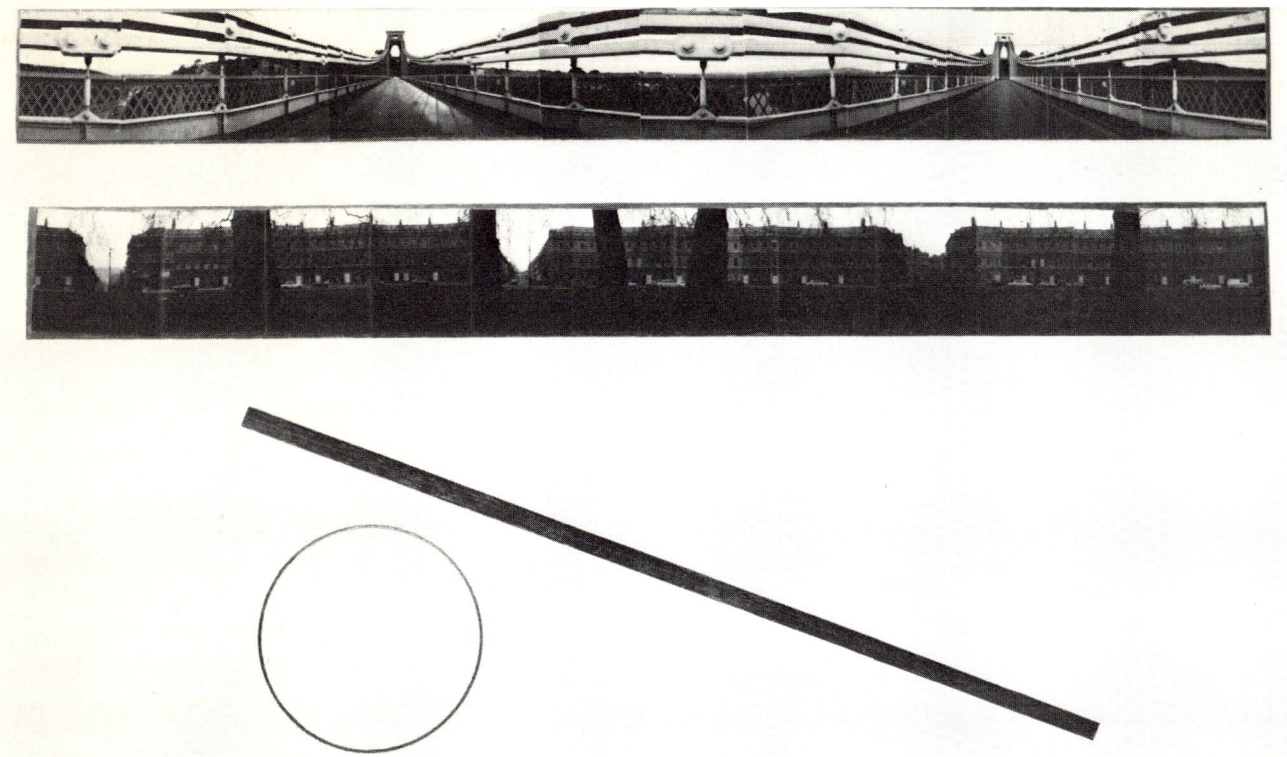

9 J. Dibbets, *A Circle and a Line*, 1976–7

One then notices that the wide, length-ways image has had an age-old use in connection with story-telling—that is, in laying out events sequentially in time. In venerated historical examples—one thinks of Trajan's Column from second century Rome or the Bayeux Tapestry—an exceedingly wide single image contains a number of scenes, the same characters recurring from part to part and a method of 'reading' being implied for the whole. During the last half of the nineteenth century artists and photographers returned to the problems of representing time in an image, and evolved techniques for capturing a rapid succession of events in a single 'strip' image running from left to right. The experiments in early cinematic procedures by Muybridge, Marey and Eakins most certainly partake in the same quest for verisimilitude which Barker had begun, and their images, too, though static, were noticeably elongated in order to symbolise temporal flow. Some of the boldest of the mid-Victorian panoramas did, indeed, consist of vast lengths of canvas which were unrolled before an audience as a means of conveying one scene after another.

Furthermore, a newly perceived relationship between space and time was one of the central facts of the art of the various 'vanguard' groups in the early years of the twentieth century; but by all accounts the actual painted panorama all but vanished from the scene during this period, not to re-emerge with any significance, until after the Second World War. One can only speculate that artistic interest in panoramic imagery became swamped by the burgeoning problems of modernity generally—particularly the problem of abstraction. And the newsreel function of the panorama had clearly gone. So had its documentary or topographical utility.

In recent times, however, the question of time and space has come back into the foreground. Perhaps it is a cliche to point out that the categories of space and time have interpenetrated each other in the sciences; but in art, the idea of *process*, which is at once both temporal and spatial, has attracted particular attention since the Second World War. Artists have explored the possibility of taking as a subject for their 'all-embracing view' not just a fragment of landscape or a scene from everyday life, but such diverse categories as natural events, the workings of a camera,

as much as the painter could see without moving his head, normally about 55 or 60 degrees of the visual field, should appear in one image. It took a Victorian artist to coin a word for the concept and to take its meaning absolutely literally, going right round the circle of the horizon[4]: and twentieth-century entertainment moguls to insist on the total sensory assault.

We are nearer the heart of the matter when we notice that the nineteenth-century panorama satisfied two cravings which were present in English culture generally. One of these was for encyclopaedic knowledge—the kind that produced such 'all-embracing' surveys as the Crystal Palace exhibition of 1851: and the other was a growing public demand for information about daily events. As Richard Altick puts it: 'Panoramas became the newsreels

of the Napoleonic era. When Robert Barker met Nelson in 1799, the admiral told him that he was indebted to him for keeping up the fame of his victory in the Battle of the Nile for a year longer than it would have lasted in the public estimation'.[5] Artists of the easel picture were swept along by this same desire to record the daily scene. William Frith, to take one of the best known examples, painted documentary pictures of his life and times in which he used the wide horizontal format as a means of maximizing the total quantity of observed detail. His *Life at the Seaside* (1852–4) is a good example of this branch of the early newsreel industry (Illustration 8). One is tempted to say that 'wide-eyed' might be the best adjective to summarize the psychology of the painted panorama during the nineteenth century.

19

10 J. Pollock, *Number Ten*, 1949

the making of an image, a journey, the human body. During the phase of conceptual-type work of the 1960's and early 1970's, a philosophical-cum-scientific attitude governed the investigations of many artists, and results tended to be diagrammatic, often black-and-white, and only coldly poetic. Muybridge's much earlier pictures provide an inescapable comparison. In the last twenty or so years abstruse questions about space and time have been researched by artists with the kind of rigour appropriate to the laboratory—and it is in this context that the panoramic format has re-appeared in an altogether new guise. Successive images have been placed together horizontally (and sometimes vertically, or in a grid) in order to 'read' together as a total elongated image, at the same time as parading the structure between their related parts. Unlike early examples of the 'image series' strictly so called, such as Monet's haystacks or cathedral facades, the more recent exponents of serial imagery have generally striven to build in *time* as an essential element of the image, just as the early cinematic experimenters did.

Of course this implies that conventions of 'reading' the image changed as well. And it is fair to say that, as with other new art forms, a host of new attitudes in the spectator were elicited by the new art of process. The spectator's reaction to, and involvement in, the aesthetic 'reading' activity itself became part of the content of the work. I think Jan Dibbets' *A Circle and a Line* (Illustration 9) provides a good general example of the 'process' approach to the panorama.

In fact of course there are sub-divisions to be made.

Firstly, a serial panorama can be made as it were additively, by putting successive images together in such a way that the time intervals between them correspond to a specified regular period. Whereas nineteenth century panoramic photographs were taken at the rate determined by the camera mechanism, the new serial works have varied the periodicity between images in all manner of ways: the result characteristically shows a wide temporal span, encompassing changes in light, atmosphere and even season within a single composite image. A second variation on the same theme is to use the movement of the artist, whether photographed or otherwise, as a parameter in the image-making process. The idea of the artist-as-part-of-his-work has fitted naturally into this general preoccupation with process, and has produced results which are still fundamentally panoramic even though appearing unfamiliar in traditional terms. The singular difference is that time and the processes of change themselves become the subject of the artist's work. And a third approach to the serial panorama has involved using a perceived subject as a unit of repetition, duplicating subjects of a like kind and stringing them together horizontally as if some strange documentary exercise were under way. All of these approaches are represented in the exhibition.

There is an interesting feature of many recent spatio-temporal panoramas which I believe should be pointed out. This is the sheer relentlessness of the process of temporal change from one moment to the next, and to the next, and to the next, which the images depict. I am struck, for instance, by how often a complete succession of temporal intervals is rendered with the monotony of a piece of machinery. The deep-rooted sense of anxiety which seems to underlie these 'serial' or 'process' works is, of course, now part of our nature. Inevitably they bring to mind the numbing rhythm of Beckett's *Watt*, in which Mr. Knott's inexorable movements are described: 'Here he moved, to and fro, from the door to the window, from the window to the door, from the window to the door, from the door to the window; from the fire to the bed, from the bed to the fire; from the bed to the fire, from the fire to the bed; from the door to the fire, from the fire to the door, from the fire to the door. . . .'[6] Mr. Knott's predicament, which is that of a person lost but still relentlessly searching, is mirrored in the more austere forms of serial art.

But the existence of these newer works should not blind us to the fact that the old-style, non-divided, elongated panoramic image is still being made by painters and photographers whose interests are more private, and less programmatically experimental. The landscape panorama in the style of Church or the Hudson River painters is evidently still a valid and serviceable form—and no less interesting for not being 'avant-garde'. Indeed the assumption of the automatic superiority of 'avant-garde' art over other forms has fallen away recently, and we have had once again to re-assess the value we place on such qualities as 'modern', 'advanced' and so forth. Hence an exhibition on a theme of this type, which cuts across schools, genres, generations and media, necessarily

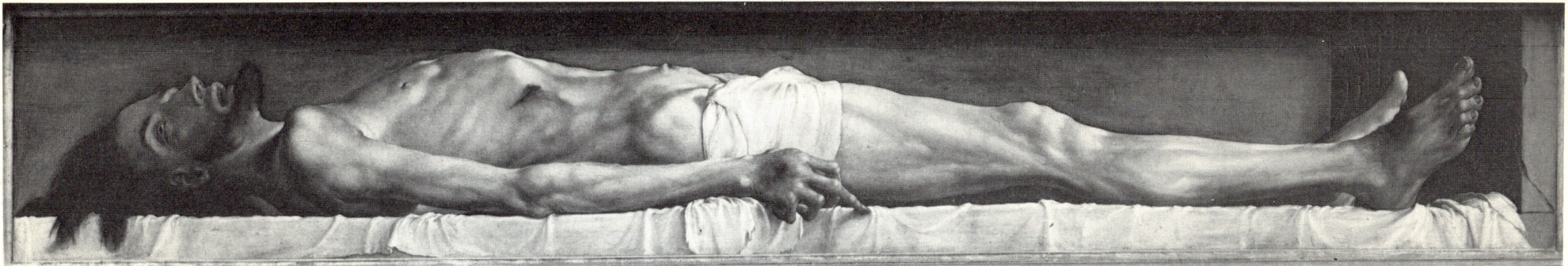

11 H. Holbein, *The Dead Christ*, 1521

contains 'traditional' and 'modern' modes alongside each other—an awkward, but also a stimulating co-mingling.

As an image-type, therefore, the panorama is very much alive. Indeed, the more we look at the panorama in art, the more we see its presence elsewhere as well. For an image-type is, after all, capable of being formed in any medium. Outside of visual art the idea of the 'all-embracing view' occurs notoriously in epic poetry where you characteristically have a magnificent sweep of events laid out in time. In the information-explosion of our own day, in which the distinction between fiction and fact has become blurred and confused, all information about all subjects, real or imaginary, is potentially co-present. Television and newspapers present such a bewildering diversity of unconnected impressions—clowns and custard pies one moment, a nuclear disaster the next—as to constitute perhaps the ultimate extension of the panoramic idea (certainly the least appetizing one).

To return to the sphere of art, finally, it is interesting to speculate on the question of what the panorama is *not*. If, as I have argued, a single image panorama must have some essential connection with the perceived world, and landscape in particular, it would seem to follow logically that abstract art will have less use for the panoramic format. Indeed I think it will be accepted that the sorts of abstract relationship which require an elongated horizontal shape are necessarily few and far between. In such cases (one thinks of Barnett Newman and Pollock), the picture is not a true panorama but becomes something else. In Pollock's *Number Ten* (1949) for instance,

(Illustration 10) the organization is essentially that of a frieze; it lacks perspective organization and contains no specifically pictorial relations. Admittedly Pollock had said in a 1944 interview that New York life was 'keener, more demanding, more intense and expansive' than in the West; but that he had a 'definite feeling for the West: the vast horizontality of the land, for instance; here (in New York) only the Atlantic Ocean gives you that'.[7] This has led commentators (especially during bicentennial year) to see Pollock and others as modern panoramic artists in the Hudson River tradition. Indeed there are many large American canvasses that come as close to Church in their general scale as you could ask. In his essay '*Big*', for instance, Harold Rosenberg identified Lee Krasner, Milton Resnick, Cy Twombly, Jules Olitski and Al Held, as well as Pollock, as exponents of what he called 'panoramic abstraction'.[8] But since these pictures tend to lack the objective or topographical element, and seldom come near to the concept of an 'all-embracing view', I think they must be excluded from our definition on every count. (Of course, the general observation that abstract pictures tend not to be panoramic does not imply that non-abstract pictures necessarily are, even given the correct shape. Holbein's *Dead Christ* of 1521, for example, although broad and low, is rendered too much in close-up to be properly panoramic (Illustration 11). It serves to remind us that there must be distance from the subject in a true panorama, even though the exact distance may be impossible to define.)

Something approaching the non-panoramic, frieze

method of composition was also employed by Courbet in his *Burial at Ornans* (1849) (Illustration 12). The horizontal layout of this great picture has been described, I think perceptively, as a kind of entreatment to socialism on earth. Linda Nochlin writes that the horizontal relationships imply 'not the ascent of man's soul to Heaven, but the joining together of men on earth in a specific and localised community, in memory of one of its members recently dead . . . the links in the chain of being are social and factual, going from one homely black-clad Ornanais to the next . . . simply aligned in an additive, horizontal procession across the canvas . . .'.[9]

The idea of egalitarianism in the sphere of social life is part and parcel of the wider materialism which gained acceptance as a world-view in the last century and which permeates the present one. We are led naturally to the thought that the long horizontal image, based upon actual perception, must also express at a fundamental level the materialistic, anti-spiritual outlook which is characteristic of the modern world. In point of fact Jung chose exactly this metaphor, of horizontality contrasted with verticality, in describing the 'obtrusive conviction that material things alone have substance' that has typified the decline of spirituality in the West. He speaks of the 'horizontal outlook of modern times' (by modern times he means the post-Reformation period in general and nineteenth century materialism in particular): 'Consciousness ceased to grow upwards, and grew instead in breadth of view, as well as in knowledge of the terrestrial globe.'[10]

Taking the positive as well as the negative points together, we are left with a general characterization of the panoramic image that runs as follows. It should attempt to capture, by means of a horizontally emphasized format, an exaggerated sense of distance in either space or time, or both. A modicum of topographical or geographical objectivity appears to be necessary as part of the 'distancing' requirement which we just observed, while too intimate a treatment can result in something closer to a subjective glimpse into another world than to an 'all-embracing view' of part of this one. With these general observations we can now turn to the artists represented in the show.

The works by Bob Chaplin included here are lyrical seascape pictures showing wide sweeps of the visual field in the Scilly Isles and the Orkneys respectively: but an unusual structure is used. Each image is composed of six sub-images, combined into two pairs of three, one set of three lying above the other in a precise and orderly arrangement. The dead-pan conjunction of High Tide with Low Tide, or, in other cases, of Sunday Morning with Sunday Evening, is partly a reflection of the 'minimal' background out of which these works come, but also a remnant of the 'conceptual' manner of thinking which was prevalent for a decade or so before 1975, in which an artist would often shift from the visual plane in order to draw attention to the verbal, propositional content of a work, and also in order to strike up an aloof and sometimes even a puritanical posture towards colour, unplanned expression or anything resembling a spontaneous outpouring.[11] Constraint and purity were the moral values which were embodied in both of those art movements and they recur here in Chaplin's work, only slightly flavoured by a discreet and gentlemanly sense of colour. You will also notice that each of the photographic images represents a moment of time which is identified by the artist. Each moment is divided from its neighbour by more or less the same amount. This is essential not only for the orderly morality of the final image, but also as an indicator of content. Time as well as space has extension. The cycle of nature is unending, inexorable and constantly repeated, but never repetitious. To take a more venerable reference point, it could be argued that

12 G. Courbet, *Burial at Ornans*, 1849

Chaplin's works also derive from the tradition of sublime landscape as practised by, say, Bierstadt or Caspar David Friedrich.

The full title of Jan Dibbets' work is 'A Circle (The Circus, John Wood 1754, Bath) and a Line (Clifton Suspension Bridge, Isambard Kingdom Brunel, 1830–1859, around Bristol). A Panorama piece photographed by me and Mr Southerne with the help of Mr Clive Adams and dedicated to Mr Richard Long, artist at Bristol'. Almost all of Dibbets' work up to the date of this piece, and much of it since, has in one way or another centred on the age-old problems of perception, of perspective, of representation, of how the subjective image can alter, and be altered by, what we (somewhat hopefully) call the objective fact. Dibbets' early 'conceptual' work consisted of a series of 'perspective corrections'; that is, visual tricks such as showing how a trapezoid on a wall might appear directly square when photographed from a specific point. His subsequent *Dutch Mountains* series consist of photographic panels joined together to create the illusion that the flat Dutch landscape was tilting or rising — merely by systematically tilting the camera with each successive frame. The work of Richard Long from the same period was clearly influential on him. *A Circle and a Line*, finished in 1977, takes as its subject the two most famous artefacts based on simple geometry in what is now the county of Avon in South West England. Dibbets transforms the straight bridge into a bending, undulating image, and turns the pure circle into what is virtually a straight line of buildings. The customary Dibbets diagram is drawn underneath; in this case a circle and a line. The reduction is complete. Of all Dibbets' panoramas this work is one of the most simple, one of the most effective, and because it is one of the least well known of Dibbets' productions, a particularly relevant inclusion in our survey of the panoramic type.

Rackstraw Downes is a rare and interesting talent. Thus far unknown in English art circles, he was born in Chichester and migrated to America in 1961 to study art at Yale after reading English at Cambridge, England. Thereafter he wrote art criticism for the New York Times.

13 R. Downes, *The Natural History Museum*, 1977

(He now writes about art, his own and others, better than any English-born artist I know.)

In one way the prototype to which *The Dam at Fairfield* (1974) belongs is Frederick Church's vista *The Niagara Falls*. But here of course is the difference; for Downes shows us instead a modest man-made river dam, a nondescript and quotidian place which is neither a beauty spot nor any kind of undiscovered view. It provides us with an excellent point of entry into Downes' art, for it is the very lack of glamour which he finds in the landscape that makes his work truly modern. Downes belongs to the ranks of unofficial American art, to those who, like Leland Bell, Rosemarie Beck, Paul Resike, and Neil Welliver were swamped into relative obscurity by the hero-mongering formalism of official thinking in the 1960s and since. I think that only Alex Katz, Downes' teacher, is well known over here, and perhaps Fairfield Porter, for his writings, which are much underrated. These 'unofficial' artists emerge from the shadows as a group who are not afraid of imagery and of observation, who do not oppose abstraction on the grounds of any dogma, but who wish, in their separate ways, to paint contemporary, real paintings with a respectful eye to the master painters of the past—in Downes' case, Van Eyck, Breughel and Theodore Rousseau in Europe, and Charles Burchfield and the Scottish

emigrant John Kane in America. In separating himself from the mainstream, Downes writes of 'Post-Modernism' that 'it has noted that a Fauve landscape smells of paint, a Barbizon one of dew. It is aware that historical accuracy and theatrical skill were unable to rescue the nineteenth century subject picture from banality; but it finds that the comprehending eye makes pertinent demands on visual invention, as it did to Van Eyck when he painted forty-two identifiable plant species on the lawn round the Altar of the Lamb, or to Breughel when he painted five clinical types of blindness in his *Blind Leading the Blind* . . . In the wake of Modernism's successes and lessons, a clean leap into holism was unlikely and a finding of various footholds has been the only conceivable procedure . . .'[12]

Thus Downes himself is an artist with an eye for every detail, every mood of weather, every sense of place. In his *Softball Practice at Skowhegan* (1975) he gives us another intriguing image. It is early evening. Nothing much is happening. People are lolling about in between strikes of a softball practice. One player has his bat raised, the rest are at ease. It is not a memorable moment or a grand event. Indeed (and this I think is the point) the painting would have been half its present self if Downes had set out to capture a spectacle. Actually the desultory scene is animated by light, by atmosphere, by season, by tempera-

ture. An apparently arbitrary moment has been captured in memory and recorded with almost photographic precision—although Downes never uses a camera and always paints, painstakingly, direct from nature. His ability to transform an apparently insignificant or even banal visual scene into a significant painted image reminds us of how Warhol managed to make interesting what we might otherwise have dismissed as boring or pointless.

The panoramic format is one which Downes has cultivated for a number of specific purposes. The suitability of this format for the wide sweep of the landscape is clear, and the wide-angle landscape was, indeed, why Downes first used the long picture. Transferring the same approach to an urban scene gives rise to many a perceptual puzzle, however, The Natural History Museum in New York is situated between 77th and 81st streets on Central Park West. Downes' painting of the *Natural History Museum* (Illustration 13) is painted from a position on the pavement at the point where 81st street (on the left of the picture) intersects at right angles with Columbus Avenue (on the right). The painting is, in effect, an experiment in realism, the conclusion of which is that realism is impossible in any absolute sense. Downes shows us that the result of turning the head to left and right to encompass an angle of around 100° produces a perspectival effect of a double kind: vertical lines on the periphery of the visual field slope back as they go upwards, while horizontal angles, such as the right angle between the streets, become diminished in the final image. Both effects ensue from the very exacting task of putting down in a panoramic format a much wider portion of the visual field than can actually be seen at any one time; the resulting painting is a single image that can be comprehended at once. The distortions are not those of the fish-eye lens, which produces a uniform bulge at the centre, but the far more subtle distortions resulting from the joint action of the human eye and memory upon fresh visual data, guided by the intention to record on a flat surface what is actually there. Since every artist comes to a scene with different memories, different mental schemata and different mechanisms of selectivity, the element of realism in Realism can only lie in the *intention* to be faithful to nature, never in the actual results. These, ironically, are destined to be highly personal constructions.

The astonishing photographic panorama of Hamish Fulton's journey in Iceland takes to an extreme the idea of nature as a sublime region, vast and awesome, in which man's place appears as being infinitesimal, even subservient, to some larger design. Despite its overall grey tonality, Fulton's multiple photograph conveys not only the drama of night and day and the cycle of nature, but its mystery and depth as well. As with Church's large painting of 1857, it also hints at the frontier of nature beyond which man has scarcely ventured.

Vaughn Gryll's massive work The Wailing Wall, Jerusalem (1979) is consistent with his other large photograph pieces done in the last few years. In each case (recent examples are The Assassination of President Kennedy (1980) and In Flanders Field (1980)) the theme is that of death. Since the international trauma of the Cuban missile crisis in 1962, Grylls has been intermittently preoccupied with the prospect of an actual holocaust, the second coming, the Millennium, the end of our civilization—the precise verbal classification is beside the point. He intends us to contemplate our own rush to destruction in each of these images. The Wailing Wall, which is itself assembled like a wall, pictures the one remaining element of Herod's temple, which was built on the site of the Temple of Solomon but which was destroyed by the Romans in the first century—with the western wall left standing to remind the Jews, and posterity, of the extent of Roman power. It is now a place of worship and remembrance, into which notes of prayer are stuck by those gathered at the base, men to the left of the screen and women segregated to the right. Grylls' image, which is composed of smaller photographs made from slides taken over the course of a few hours, is virtually a documentary photograph blown up extremely large, with none of the conceits of art or sophisticated technique. There is the place—and here is our life. We should remember our mortality (Grylls is saying) and prepare ourselves for death.

The majority of John Hilliard's art over the last ten years has consisted of using photography to reveal aspects of the camera as a recording device which might otherwise have remained hidden. He has certainly exploited the serial layout, either the horizontal sequence or the grid, in original ways. Hilliard's work, Sixty Seconds of Light (2) (1970) for instance, consisted of an intentionally dead-pan array of twelve shots of the same clock, each one taken with a different exposure which shows the clock's second hand at different positions on the dial. It demonstrated by means of a photograph the way in which the camera makes a photograph; and it also showed how the camera can alter what it depicts, depending on its internal programming of aperture, focus, exposure. The work in this exhibition is the third version of Ten Runs Past a Fixed Point, the first of which showed a sequence of ten photographs of a landscape subject taken at different exposures and becoming successively more blurred and abstracted, and the second of which showed a similar sequence, but this time with a man literally running past the starting point in the photograph while the camera remained still.[13] The third version develops the theme. Each panel contains a pair of photographs, the top one being of the stationary camera which photographs the running man (Hilliard himself) and the lower one being of the running man who photographs the stationary camera. Thus each photograph refers to the other. The sequence as a whole, consisting of exposures from 1/500th to 1 second, goes from the dark of the under-exposed panel on the far left, through 'normal' exposures in the centre, to the blurred white form of the panel on the farthest right. It is a striking image, showing the panoramic format put to original use in photographic analysis of the most clinical kind.

Ivon Hitchens for the most part worked at the borders of naturalism, where it passes over into abstraction. He reached more or less the same point as Kandinsky did in his early abstract landscapes, but without Kandinsky's mysticism. Likewise a strong vein of nature-identification is present in Hitchens' work, but not the overtly spiritual, other-worldly kind which early European modernists cultivated, or even the kind of nature-mysticism developed by Hitchens' English contemporary Paul Nash. The majority of Hitchens' painting was done in the South of England, and since 1940 much of it in West Sussex. The elongated horizontal canvas first appeared in his work in the 1930's and became virtually standard during the 1940's. The idea was to free 'the natural flow of horizontals'[14] within the picture, to give a sense of the earth as a shape, and to provide a convenient vehicle for the generally fluid and mobile conception of nature which Hitchens saw. Form is always presented in terms of soft, limpid patches of paint, fixed carefully in position yet without giving the look of being attached or static. Giant Oak Tree and Open Sky (1978) contains a number of notable Hitchens features. The painting is divided vertically into regions, each with its own perspective, and yet each flowing into the next (this became an axiom of cubist painting theory after 1908, although the same device can be seen in embryonic form in Constable). Within this structure nature is made to wash about in the sea of her own colour. Uninhabited by people, such paintings are nevertheless full of the life-force of nature and hence without any need for human life. There is generally some distance from the subject, too, which is what confirms Hitchens as a panoramist. But at the same time, the psychological identification between artist and scene makes the distance between them shrink to zero; in the final analysis they are one and the same.

John Loker's painting in the present show is one of a number of landscape works which have developed organically out of an earlier interest in very long, horizontal, three-dimensional wall constructions and floor sculptures. They consist of elongated landscape images 'banked' one above the other, making up a total image running in serial form either from the bottom up, or from the top down. In most of Loker's work the top image, which occupies less vertical space, is larger in detail and in grid size than the lower ones, and this creates a reversal of ordinary vision, in which the higher detail is smaller. It is as if we were shifting into closer focus with each successive image. In Vertical Extracts, however, this convention is reversed, and the visual flow is un-ambiguously downwards, from the top. The images themselves are curious. Although there is landscape detail present, and although each sub-image is spread out horizontally in the characteristic panoramic format, in the last analysis the painting itself is only marginally about landscape as we experience it. The marks on the painting are taken from a source in the landscape, and then developed from a central cluster on the painting surface, spreading outwards to the edges, and shifted to right or left with the change to the larger or smaller version which is above or below. The process of perceptual scanning is converted into a constructional device; thus Loker's paintings are really manifestations of painting technique, with landscape as the pretext. The colours, too, are delicate and soft, and set the mood of the painting. The slow, deliberate changes of focus are relaxed and systematic, like poetry which is quiet and simple.

15 S. Shatter, *View of Brooklyn*, 1978

14 R. Long, *A Six Day Walk Centred on Cerne Abbas*, 1975

Richard Long has travelled to every part of the world in pursuit of his art. He might rearrange the stones on a mountainside in the Himalayas, lay down pieces of stick in a certain order, or simply walk in a series of geometrically precise circles round a fixed point. The results, carefully recorded on maps or photographed in a romantic manner, embody the results of these activities in visual form. Being neither painting nor sculpture, they record a human being's efforts to impose a simple order (whether in the form of a circle or a square or another basic figure) on a disorderly and random nature. Most of his works are sparse and sometimes puritanical in conception, and attempt to convey in the simplest possible statement the bare facts of human intervention in remote little-known places. The work illustrated in this catalogue and the exhibited piece are both panoramic in conception, being concerned in one way or another with an 'all-embracing view' of a natural scene. The *Six Day Walk Centred on Cerne Abbas*, (1975) (Illustration 14) shows us the artist, insect-like, as a meticulous searcher-out of detail. The paths fan out from Cerne Abbas like lines of energy radiating from a point. It is as if the memory of a place were being constructed in minute detail according to an elaborate and painstaking ritual, and embodied finally in a strikingly iconic 'mandala' image. A similar procedure has been adopted for *A 2½ Day Circular Walk in the Scottish Highlands* (1979) but with dissimilar results. Here the image is sparser still, to the point where it has all but vanished.[15] So, also, has the autograph of the artist. The work is painted onto the wall by a signwriter to given instructions, and then destroyed after the exhibition— hence in theory the work can be repeated and duplicated ad infinitum. Showing neither view nor atmosphere, it merely records the bare essentials of a long circular walk in an unknown place at an unknown time. Long has forfeited image-making in order to capitalize on the mute, silent, nearly mystical offering. This is really landscape converted into haiku.

Ed Ruscha's work selected for this exhibition, two silkscreen prints from 1978 (entitled *I've Never Seen Two People Looking Healthier* and *Let's Keep in Touch*) and the twenty-seven foot long fold-out book *Every Building on Sunset Strip* (1966) illustrate different phases of this artist's work. In some ways they summarize the different outlooks which corresponded to two different decades. The earlier work is really an act of homage to California's two most famous possessions, Sunset Strip in Los Angeles and the motor car; the image shows the former by means

16 Hamish Fulton (1975)

derived from the motion of the latter. In a sense it also epitomises the 'serial' approach to the panoramic image. Each building is represented as equal in status to every other—and implicitly equal in interest and value. At the same time this is one of the hallmarks of the cult of the banal and corny that still characterises West Coast art: no distinction is made between 'kitsch' and 'real' exemplars of any type. Everything is depicted as being equally valid or worthy of attention—perhaps the only exception being that which had thus far escaped attention. In the case of the two silk-screen prints, however, Ruscha's wit has taken quite another form. These works are combinations of visual image and verbal cliche, resulting in a comment which is both wry and oblique. They are also masterfully executed. The considerable width of the image, combined with the 'long distance' viewpoint and small detail, give both works that element of false pretension which is necessary for the success of the joke.

Susan Shatter is an American artist who has made a strong impression with her panoramic paintings on the other side of the Atlantic. This is her first exhibition in England. Her pictures are not always panoramic, although the very large *View of Brooklyn* illustrated here (Illustration 15) is a typical example of one which is. Sometimes painted from observation but more generally done from photographs, these pictures show the visual span of the urban landscape as spreading itself out across the field of vision. The high view point of the Manhattan pictures particularly recalls Durer's battle-scene. In fact, to judge from Susan Shatter's pictures of Boston and her landscape works of the Grand Canyon, she seems to like to look down on her subjects—a fact presumably of some personal significance. These two smaller watercolours in our exhibition are more intimate and reflective. In some ways they stand alongside Ivon Hitchens' Sussex landscapes in mood and in format, but without the gusto of Hitchens' images. Or again, the comparison might be Durer's soft, quiescent watercolours of the 1490s. It is unlikely, however, that a European artist would ever 'go to such lengths' in the elongation of his work as we find in Susan Shatter's American paintings.[16]

Brandon Taylor

Notes

(1) Henry T. Tuckerman, *Book of the Artists* (1867: reprint, New York, James F. Carr, 1966) p. 376.
(2) An excellent account of the early panoramas can be found in Richard Altick's compendious new book *The Shows of London* (Harvard University Press, 1978) to which I am much indebted. Altick also points out (p. 132) that Barker had known both Trumbull and Benjamin West, the former having asked Barker to convert some sketches of Niagara Falls into a panorama as early as 1808.
(3) W. Dunlap, *A History of the Rise and Progress of the Arts of Design in the United States* (ed. F. W. Bayley and C. E. Goodspeed, Boston, 1918) I, pp. 315–6.
(4) The psychological significance of the *circularity* of panoramic presentations is not something I have the space to explore here. An indispensable text is C. G. Jung's Concerning Mandala Symbolism (1950) *Collected Works* Vol. 9.
(5) Altick, *op. cit.*, p. 136.
(6) S. Becket, *Watt*, Calder Jupiter Books, 1963, p. 203.
(7) 'Jackson Pollock', *Art and Architecture*, Los Angeles, February 1944, p. 14.
(8) H. Rosenberg, *Artworks and Packages*, Delta, 1969, pp. 113–123.
(9) Linda Nochlin, *Realism*, (Penguin Books, 1971), p. 81.
(12) Rackstraw Downes, Post-Modernist Painting, *Tracks*, Fall, 1976.
(10) C. G. Jung, Basic Postulates of Analytical Psychology: first published as Die Entschleierung der Seele in *Europäische Revue*, July 1931.
(11) In this connection, see Brandon Taylor, Textual Art (in catalogue to 'Artists Books', Arts Council of Great Britain, 1976).
(12) Rackstraw Downes, Post-Modernist Paintings, *Tracks*, Fall 1976.
(13) The first two versions are reproduced in *Studio International*, April 1972, pp. 168–9.
(14) See Mary Sorrell's article 'Ivon Hitchens', *The Listener* April 1947.
(15) See also Long's A Straight Northward Walk across Dartmoor, reproduced in *Aggie Weston's Magazine*, No. 16, 1979.

The Panoramic Image in Photography

'We shouldn't pretend that panoramas are intrinsically interesting—only that given the grey drabness of the majority there are some pleasant surprises.'
Simon Nathan—Simon Wide Photographs

Panoramic photography is a fascinating but much neglected area. The aim of this section of the exhibition is not just to show the wide variety of the photographic panorama or its historic scope but, more important, to show some of the 'pleasant surprises'—the better, more interesting examples of the genre.

It is not easy to say why panoramas were taken, who used them, who enjoyed them and for what reasons. We can only make generalizations from numerous but possibly unrepresentative survivals. Like the broader field of photography itself, early panoramas were a novelty and as such were a success; they also adequately served a number of more strictly commercial functions. A quick overview of the development of panoramic photography seems to show that the bulk of the nineteenth century work is commercially orientated—few showing what we might today call any deliberate 'aesthetic' impulse on the part of the photographer. At the turn of the century panoramas went 'popular', that is, became readily available to the public at large with the development of a hand-held camera using more convenient roll-film. In the 1930's, and even more so in the post World War II period, there was a rediscovery of the panorama and an exploration of it as an 'art' medium, a means to express a more personal vision and to extend the visual vocabulary. Its use as a documentary medium continued, but this area, too, was re-interpreted and more consciously incorporated into the current body of photographic aesthetics.

During the first years of photography generally, there was an incredible curiosity about new ways of seeing and new technical means of taking pictures. It is not surprising, therefore, that within the first ten years following the 'birth of photography'[1] there were not only pieced-together panoramas but an actual panoramic camera.[2] In 1842 Antoine F. J. Claudet took a panoramic series of London, a full 360 degree coverage from the top of the Duke of York Column in Pall Mall. An engraving made from the photographs was published in 1843 and billed as a 'picture bigger than anything previously issued',—it measured $36'' \times 50''$.[3] As early as 1843 W. H. Fox Talbot was producing a number of panoramas made up of a sequence of prints. Indeed, many of his photos hitherto accepted as single images turn out to be sections of panoramas, with marks on them indicating the overlap for joining them together. (This oversight occurred because at an early stage Talbot's photographs had been divided and placed into diverse collections.) Meanwhile, Friedrich von Martens, a German living in Paris, in 1844 made the first working panoramic camera, one using the daguerreotype process. Thereafter a spate of cameras, more or less panoramic, were described, patented or actually built and sold.

The development of the whole field of panoramic photography seemed to be spurred on by Victorian ingenuity and the Victorians' penchant for invention and gadgetry. Certainly the numerous developments in other areas of photography pointed to their constant quest for novelty. There was a remarkable desire to produce the 'biggest', 'largest' or 'greatest' photograph or camera. This led to some bizarre excesses. The greatest accolade appeared to be that the picture left the viewer 'breathless'.

17 F. J. Schlueter, *Goose Creek Oil Field, Texas,* 1919

To this end, in 1867, a 35-foot long panorama was made of the Krupps steel works. This was not only a remarkably long image but was made up of individual prints that were $22'' \times 26''$, a rather large format.[4] Charles Bayliss and Bernard Otto Halterman made a 30-foot long panorama of Sydney in 1867, and theirs were the largest wet plate negatives ever made, each being $3\frac{1}{2}' \times 5'$. The camera was mounted on a specially built tower 74 feet high and had a $100''$ focal length lens that was 10 feet long.[5] An R. Thiele in Moscow in 1903 constructed a combination of seven cameras for panoramas to be made from balloons,[6] while in the same year appeared the incredible 'Kilometer-Photographie', or so the process was nicknamed. The perpetrators of this were the Neue Photographische Gesellschaft of Berlin who naturally boasted it as the 'largest' picture in the world being a $5' \times 39'$ view of the Gulf of Naples on one continuous sheet of paper (though made from separate negatives). To produce one print required that tanks specifically be made for developing and fixing the print and a small railway track built to shift them, while the tank for washing was $50' \times 6\frac{1}{2}' \times 2\frac{1}{2}'$. As there was no darkroom available that was large enough in which to work, the printing was done outdoors at night. The exposed paper was wound on a wooden wheel 41 feet in circumference which was lowered into the respective tanks and rotated.[7]

The panoramic photograph was part of a continuous search for things that amused or astounded, whether by having something different, or bigger, or wider, or just something that showed 'more'. In this realm of entertainment a direct link can be seen between the panoramic photograph and its precursors: painted panoramas and the Diorama. Such an association is made even more appealing because Daguerre himself collaborated as a youth on many panoramic paintings and invented the Diorama as an improved version of this form of theatre—but he himself is not known to have taken a panoramic photograph.

Photography was a logical continuation of both in that it was another means of casting a visual spell and producing an illusion of reality. The connection was not so much the similarity, in the attempts at size or wideness, between the painted panorama and the photographic one,

but in the social needs they served to satisfy. Altick points out that such shows ministered to the 'desire to be amused or instructed, the indulgence of curiosity and a sheer sense of wonder, sometimes a rudimentary aesthetic sensibility'.[8] They were a 'supplement to books, particularly to illustrate in tangible form some of the most popular kinds of informational literature . . .: narratives of exploration and travel . . ., treatises on pseudo-science and science . . ., and histories (including the stories of momentous recent events).[9] There was the element of journalism, to illustrate history as it was being made—at that time mostly expeditions and explorations of distant lands. Common to both photographic and painted panoramas was the tendency to show scenes of 'intrinsic interest by virtue of their exoticism, publicized picturesqueness or historical association'.[10] Certainly there was in both an insistence on topographical accuracy—; verisimilitude being a basic principle of nineteenth century English aesthetic doctrine. Nor is the power of the panoramic concept dead as witness latter day forms in Cinerama or Panavision.

Verisimilitude was the keynote, and early panoramas served mainly to make a record, to document and register events and occasions. Most panoramic photographs were taken by commercial photographers whose output ranged from taking school or military 'class' pictures, to recording oil fields (labelling each derrick), logging activities, factories, mining and indeed any type of industry, frontier towns, the construction of railways and the opening up of new lands in general. In the United States there were even a number of itinerant panoramists who just photographed the main streets of small towns, particularly in the Midwest: the same picture, almost, hundreds of times over. Crowds were a perennial favourite, at sporting events, rallies, conventions, banquets; group shots taken for the record and for commercial gain. The genre becomes so predictable that one chuckles with relief when one sees some small variant. At rare times a picture rises above the general level of routine photography and stands out as an image in its own right, fascinating, charming, and drawing one into the mysteries of the past.

Naturally, the panorama was suited to the number of firms whose purpose was to sell views to the public of well-

known and much visited tourist spots, both at home and abroad. Most commercial view makers made it a practice to have a number of different formats and types of camera to take each scenic spot at the same time. Thus the public were able to buy a print for an album or a larger one for the wall or a stereoscopic one for after dinner entertainment. Occasionally such a photographer would take a series of shots for a pieced-together panorama; Felice Beato often did this. Some, like Adolph Braun senior, actually had a panoramic camera as part of their regular equipment (his was a Johnson's Pantoscopic).

The landscape, too, was 'recorded', the panorama being the ideal format to make the most complete topographical record. The nineteenth century was addicted to 'scientific accuracy', and Aimé Civiale's aims, for instance, were avowedly 'scientific' when, for ten years from 1859 to 1869, he made a detailed record of the entire Alps. This was published in 1882 with 41 panoramic views,[11] an early forerunner of the NASA photographs mapping the surface of the moon.

Around 1900, with the advent of the easily portable panoramic camera that used roll film that was far more convenient than heavy and bulky plate film, the panorama became more accessible to, and was more widely used by, the general public. Such cameras as the Al-Vista and the Kodak Panoram were like box brownies, and around this time a number of albums appear of panoramic snapshots. Even the Tsarina, wife of Nicholas II, was an ardent user of the Kodak Panoram, and her album showing court life behind the scenes and public events from the 'other side' consists of a fascinating series of panoramas. An album similar to this is The Monte Carlo album which, although probably a Kodak sample album, or possibly an album made up for sale with photographs taken by company employees or commissioned from photographers, exemplifies the growing snapshot ethic as well as the freshness and occasional charm of such images.

As modern photographers broke away from the recording aspect of panoramas and used the genre to create images for their own sake, they concentrated, and capitalized more, on the abstract elements that the panorama seemed to epitomize. They conceptualized its

18 Schutz, *General Pershing and Major General Dickman with the Officers and Men of the 2nd Division, Valendar, Germany*, March 1919

particular relations to the problems of time, space, perspective, distortion or the happy accident.

The early panoramist's characteristic viewpoint was that of surveying a wide outdoor tract from a commanding eminence. But where their panoramas enhanced the magnitude of the subject, contemporary panoramists have tended to concentrate on crowded scenes and enclosed spaces; juxtaposing fine detail and intimate coverage with the panorama's natural tendency to imply wide space. A tension is set up between the small and mundane and the natural willingness to see in the panorama magnitude and grandeur. They have sought new vantage points but ones that disorientate the viewer rather than provide novelty; they work more indoors looking through spaces of various confinements and distances from the camera, using the distortion to contradict the realities of the space rather than to emphasize them.

The fact that many events could occur in the time it takes the camera, or lens, to traverse the scene it is recording leads to the deliberate incorporation of a sequential performance in the single picture; a cinema in stills, so to say. Using the principle that a person at one end of a class photo could run to the other end of the group and so appear in the photograph twice, the contemporary photographer makes this concept the sole end of the picture and ignores its primary function. Oscar Bailey's

Backyard Event, No. 2 (cat. no. 53) places the emphasis on the event of his strip, not on the backyard. Similarly, instead of pasting together the segments of a panorama in their proper order, the picture can be shown out of sequence. The viewer knows or suspects the existence of the panoramic whole and order but must struggle to overcome his disorientation, add up the pieces mentally to comprehend the totality (producing an *angst* similar to that experienced when trying to tot up a long list of numbers in one's head). Such an approach heightens the viewer's awareness of both the time sequence and the space sequence. Though the picture is disjunctive, the idea of panorama is enhanced. In an overall sense, the early portrayals of 'scenes' become portrayals of 'actions', conceptually as well as literally.

Because traditional panoramas tend to be all-encompassing and non-discriminatory in their display of detail, contemporary photographers have sought to emphasize the event, concentrating on diverse bits of detail to focus the viewer's attention instead of letting it wander at will over the picture surface. David Avison is ostensibly concerned with the component actions and additive detail of a ball game in *Central Park* (cat. no. 50) but it is a specific detail, that of a face on a carrier bag in the foreground that makes the picture.

Possibly the most disturbing aspect of panoramas is their distortion of space. It is an unconventional space,

and modern photographers have capitalized on the panorama's tendency to dislocate the scale and the volume of the scene photographed. (There is less apparent distortion if the camera is kept aligned with the horizon, and some cameras show less distortion if their lenses are more telescopic than wide-angle.)

Other attempts have been made to vary and make more interesting the straight panorama, and these coincide with a general trend in photography to revive older photographic processes and include hand-colouring, the use of cyanotype and gum-bichromate prints. No longer is size or novelty the aim of panoramas but rather the presentation of a visual idea that expresses the photographer's viewpoint. Straight record shots continue to be made, and a number are included in the show to demonstrate that these can be done with imagination and that the search for topographical record making, albeit more of the urban landscape, is not dead.

Types of panorama and the cameras used

It is precisely when one tries to define 'panorama' that one finds there is no precise definition. We have made the assumption that the panorama is a horizontal concept and therefore have chosen to show only horizontal images (though it is obvious that one can turn the panoramic camera on its side and take a vertical picture, say, of tall buildings, trees, or a waterfall, as has often been done) and assumed that it's a continuous unbroken view which can be seen from a single fixed point. None the less, we have included some exceptions, if only to prove the rule: the rearranged sequences, the slightly shifting viewpoint — all being predicated on the basic definition.

It is, furthermore, impossible to draw the line between a mere wide-angle photograph and one that is a panorama. A camera was generally considered panoramic if it or its lens covered an angle of at least 120 degrees, but more usually it covered anything over 150 degrees and up to — or even over — 360 degrees. (Potentially, of course, one could keep going round and round.)

There are basically four ways of making a panoramic photograph, with any number of variations introduced by inventors and photographers trying to improve or adapt equipment to their own purposes. Briefly, they can be classed as follows: (1) made up of pieced-together images; (2) made with a camera with a moving lens and a fixed film plane; (3) made with a camera where both the body and the film moves, and (4) made with a camera with a fixed wide-angle lens and a fixed film plane.

Pieced together. The easiest way of making a panorama without specially designed equipment is to set up a camera (in the early days usually an $8'' \times 10''$ plate camera) on a levelled tripod and to take a consecutive sequence of shots. After each shot the camera is rotated so that the next picture slightly overlaps the previous one, paying particular attention to evenness of exposure and development, so that each print will match in tone as well as in image. The final prints can be pasted together — 2, 3, 4 up to 10 or more — to make a panoramic view that can encompass up to or over 360 degrees. (Many photographers went over to include the same object on each end of the picture, so proving they had swept around the entire circle.) Such panoramas were made from almost the very beginnings of photography. Fox-Talbot in 1843 used his calotype process to take a number of them. And, although the paper calotype was easier to handle, daguerreotypists were not deterred from working in a more intractable material: a panorama made up of eight daguerreotype plates was made of the Cincinnati, Ohio, waterfront in 1848 by Charles Fontayne and W. S. Porter that has been described as spectacular.[12]

Moving lens. In 1844 Friedrich von Martens designed what is considered to be the first panoramic camera. It had a rotating lens to take panoramas on cylindrically curved metal plates. These daguerreotypes, mostly rooftop views of Paris, were $4.7'' \times 15''$ and subtended an angle of 150 degrees. The obvious drawback of von Martens' Megaskop-Kamera was the handling of a curved metal plate. The camera remained stationary while the pivoted lens encased in a flexible cloth 'bellows' or curtain was rotated by clock-work machinery.[13] A metal tube was fixed to the lens and led back to the film. At the film-plane end the tube was flattened to form a vertical slit, so that as the lens rotated, the flattened tube swept past the film and only that portion of the film directly behind the lens was exposed. This incremental exposure served to prevent fogging and distortion. The system was easily adapted a few years later for wet plate photography on curved glass, as well as for paper negatives and was ideally suited for the new roll films. A number of cameras used the rotating lens and curved film plane, including the Cylindrograph, the Al-Vista, and the Kodak Panoram. The curvature of the film helped prevent distortion of the image as, in effect, it kept the film plane always perpendicular to the portion of the scene being photographed. Ideally, to keep this loss of distortion, the image should be printed on to a curved surface and so viewed. The Al-Vista camera which appeared in 1898 was the first panoramic camera to be widely sold and provided the general public with a convenient, hand-held apparatus. Much of the convenience was due to the use of flexible silver bromide roll film that was $5''$ wide. The popular Kodak Panoram No. 4 appeared in 1899 using even smaller film $3\frac{1}{2}''$ wide. It, too, used a sweeping lens but replaced the flattened tube affixed to it by a slitted focal plane shutter that passed in front of the film synchronously with the movement of the lens. Today such cameras as the Widelux use 35 mm film which allows 21 pictures ($1'' \times 2\frac{1}{3}''$) to be taken on the normal 36-exposure roll. Most modern cameras, such as the Widelux, also employ a flat film plane thus giving more of the panoramic distortion, in which the curvature of any horizontal line that is off the horizontal axis causes the picture to appear to bulge forward in the middle.

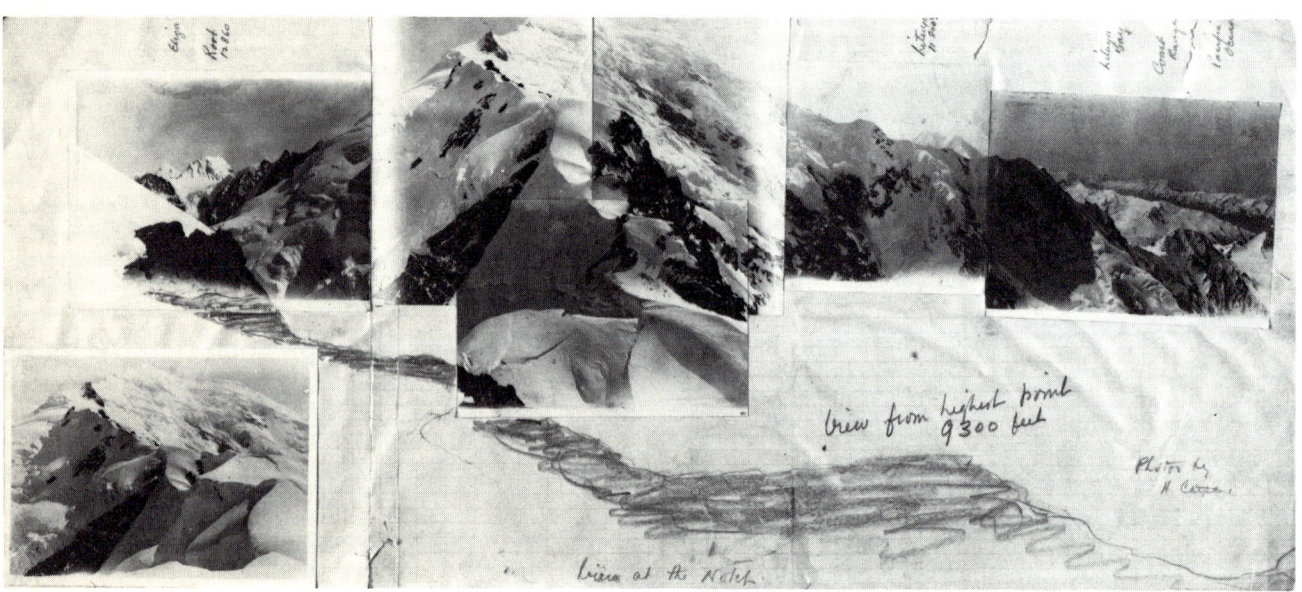

19 A. Carpe, *Mt. Fairweather*, Alaska, n.d.

20. (top and bottom)
A Kodak Panoram.

21. (top and bottom) A Kodak Cirkut, showing cogwheels (top) used in gearing, to change speed at which the turntable could rotate.

Moving camera body and moving film. In this third method, the camera rotates in one direction while the film is moved in a counter direction. The first commercial camera of this type, Johnson and Harrison's Pantoscopic of 1862, was rotated on a turntable, again by a clockwork drive, its speed regulated by a vane governor, while a plate holder with a 7.5″ × 12″ wet collodion plate was slid past a vertical slot behind the lens by the same machinery. Cannon's Wonder Panoramic and Damoizeau's Cyclograph of 1889 operated on this principle but used roll film instead of plates, with the clockwork that could turn the camera through 360 degrees simultaneously winding the film in the opposite direction. An eccentric variation of this type of camera was Lumiere's Periphot of 1901. Here

the film was held stationary around a cylinder in the centre of the camera while the entire outer body, in the shape of a drum with a lens and prism attached at right angles, like a periscope, rotated about the film. The best known and most used camera of this type was the Cirkut patented in 1904. Initially made by the Rochester Panoramic Company, it was continued by Kodak and marketed up to 1941. It was the familiar standard camera used for large group photographs such as class portraits. The speed of the camera's rotation was governed by changing the size of a cog wheel in the gearing and its generally slow speed of rotation allowed the familiar trick of having the photographer, or any other person, stand first at one end of the group and then run to stand at the

other end before the camera had completed its full sweep.
Wide-angle lens. The fixed lens, fixed film plane panoramic camera relied on a specially designed wide-angle lens. The first of this type was the Ross Panoramic fitted with Sutton's Panoramic Water lens, which covered an angle of approximately 120 degrees. The camera took curved glass collodion plates, and Sutton was able to demonstrate how the curved negatives could be printed on paper using a curved printing frame. Later, wide format cameras, generically known as banquet cameras, became quite common for pictures of large gatherings. The first was the Falmer and Schwing Banquet camera which appeared in 1913. Present day photographers have developed variations on the banquet camera to suit their own purposes. Art Sinsabaugh has been able to compress the panoramic space with his modifications, much as a telephoto lens does, rather than have it 'expand' in the usual way. Beyond this, the category of panorama becomes more diffuse, ranging from the panoramic wide angle of the banquet camera to other cameras designed for wide-angle photography such as the Kodak Wide Angle, the Agifold Envoy Wide Angle and the Panon Super Wide Angle, as well as the pinhole camera and fish-eye lenses.

It would be remiss not to mention some of the other variations on the panoramic camera, if only to show the Victorians' inventiveness and ingenuity as well as their creativity with names. Ross of New York (not the same Ross whose camera used Sutton's water lens) made a camera in 1858 called a Scioptic, or variously a Scioptric, which produced a 120-degree panorama on three glass plates. A panoramic camera called a Cyclograph (not to be confused with Damoizeau's camera of the same name) was designed by a A. H. Smith to photograph the outer surface of a cylindrical object, such as a vase, on to a flat plate. The object was placed on a circular platform which travelled along a straight guide at right angles to the lens and as it went along the object was revolved on the turntable. At the same time a screen with a vertical slit and the camera behind it travelled parallel to, and at the same speed as the object so that each successive portion of the object was exposed at the point it was nearest to the lens. The Oroheliograph was designed by Noë for taking a photograph of the entire horizon at one time—without a thing moving. The lens pointed upwards and the film plate lay horizontally beneath it. Over the lens hung, like a cone, a convex paraboloid mirror (that is, with a circular cross section and a parabolic vertical section) which reflected the view of all surrounding objects downwards to the lens; and this formed a circular image on the plate. Such views although distorted and of inconvenient format, were considered 'useful for checking surveying and photogrammetric observations'.[14]

Least, but not last, a tiny moving-lens camera called the Pigeon Panoramic was developed in 1912 to be strapped to the breast of a carrier pigeon with the shutter set off by a timing device while the pigeon was, hopefully, in flight.

Jonathan Bayer

Sources for types of Panoramic Photographs and Cameras

Brian Coe, *Cameras: From Daguerreotypes to Instant Pictures*, London, Marshal Cavendish, 1978 (Chapter 15).

Michael Auer, *The Illustrated History of the Camera: from 1839 to the Present*, translated and adapted by D. B. Tubbs, Boston, New York Graphics Society, 1975.

Cassell's Cyclopedia of Photography, ed. Bernard E. Jones, London, New York, Toronto and Melbourne, Cassell & Co. Ltd., 1911.

A. Brothers, *Photography: Its History, Processes, Apparatus and Materials*, London, Charles Griffin and Co. Ltd., 1899.

Diane Edkins, 'An Introduction to Panoramic Photography', *Panoramic Photography* catalogue, Grey Art Gallery and Study Center, New York University Faculty of Arts and Science, 1977.

'A Wide Eyed Look at Panoramic Photography', Kodak International Photography, No. 13, 1975.

Josef Maria Eder, *Ausführliches Handbuch der Photographie*, Halle A/s, Verlag von Wilhelm Knapp, 1884.

Josef Maria Eder, translated by Edward Epstean, *History of Photography*, New York, Columbia University Press, 1945.

Helmut and Alison Gernsheim, 'The History of Photography', London, Thames and Hudson, 1969.

Eaton, S. Lothrop. *A Century of Cameras*, New York, Morgan and Morgan, Inc., 1973.

Notes

(1) 1835, if one takes Talbot's earliest surviving paper negative, or 1837, if one prefers Daguerre's perfection of his 'first practical' photographic process.

(2) See below for a description of the basic ways of making a panoramic image.

22 Gerald Incandela, *Old New York*, 1978

(3) The engraving was announced in the *Illustrated London News* on 14 May, 1842, as a promotional effort to be given to those who took out a six-month subscription. Helmut and Alison Gernsheim, *The History of Photography*, 1969, p. 142.

(4) *Ibid*, pp. 316–7.

(5) *Ibid*, pp. 316–7.

(6) Josef Maria Eder, History of Photography, 1945, p. 396.

(7) Gernsheim, *op. cit.*, p. 317.

(8) Richard Altick, *The Shows of London*, 1978, p. 1.

(9) *Ibid*, p. 1.

(10) *Ibid*, pp. 176–8, *inter alia*.

(11) *Les Alpes au point de vue de la Geographie Physique de la Geologie*, *Voyages Photographiques*, Paris, 1882. Cited in Gernsheim, *op. cit.*, p. 142.

(12) Sources that have been used *inter alia* from this section are listed above in the bibliography. Particularly useful are Brian Coe and Michael Auer for a fuller illustration of the cameras and their operation.

(13) Brian Coe, *Cameras*, 1978, p. 169.

(14) *Cassell's Cyclopedia of Photography*, 1911.

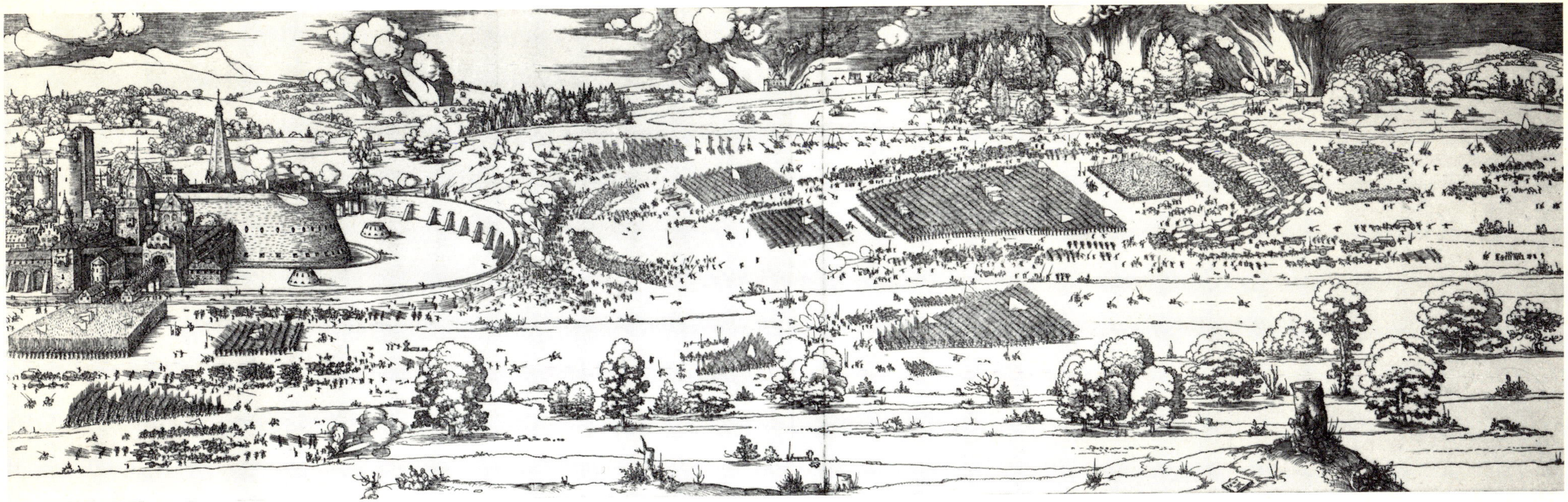

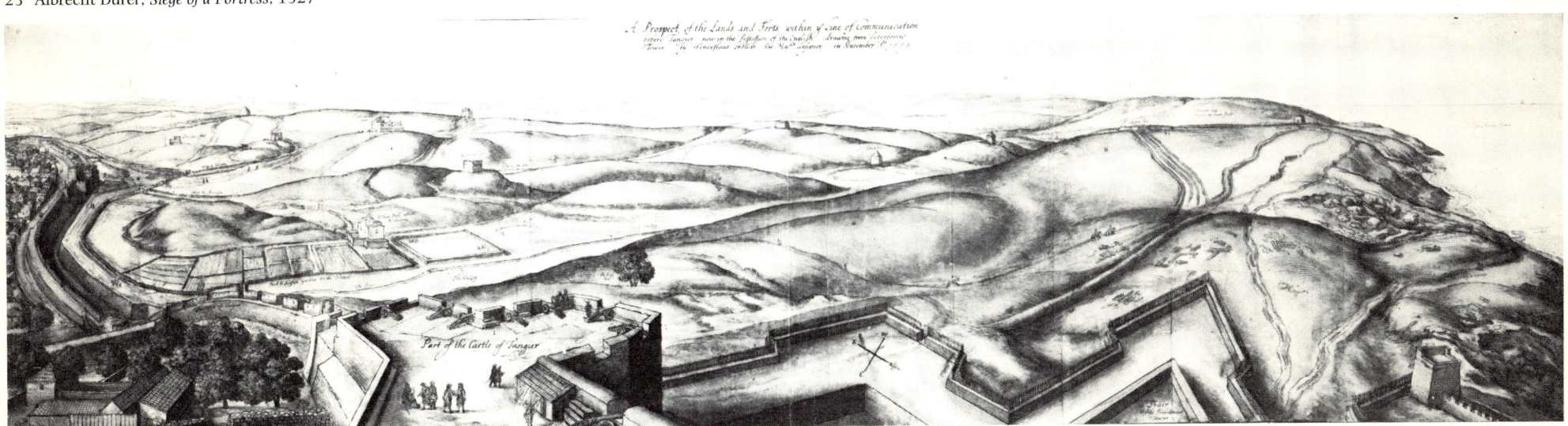

23 Albrecht Dürer, *Siege of a Fortress*, 1527

24 Wenceslaus Hollar, *Tangier from Peterborough Tower*, 1669

25 Henry Aston Barker, *Section from panorama of Paris*, 1802

26 David Roberts, *Panoramic View of Cairo*, 1839

27 Decimus Burton, *The Colosseum, Regent's Park, c.* 1822

28 Rudolf Ackermann, *View of London from a Painter's Platform* (Colosseum), 1829

29 Sir George Scharf, *The Bavarian Alps from the edge of Munich*, 1846

30 Hughes Company, *Western Maryland Dairy*, n.d.

31 R. J. Waters, *The Burning City, San Francisco*, 10 a.m., April 18, 1906

32 William Rider-Rider, *Troops of the 3rd Canadian Division*, November 1917

33 F. J. Bandholts, *Albia, Iowa*, 1907

34 Photographer Unidentified, *Monte Carlo Album, c.* 1910

35 E. O. Goldbeck, *Third Annual Bathing Girl Revue, Galveston, Texas*, May 14, 1

3RD ANNUAL
BATHING GIRL REVUE
GALVESTON TEX.
MAY 14TH 1922.

© E.O. GOLDBECK
B.A. TEXAS.

36 Eric Renner, *Ice House, Ticul, Mexico*, 1969

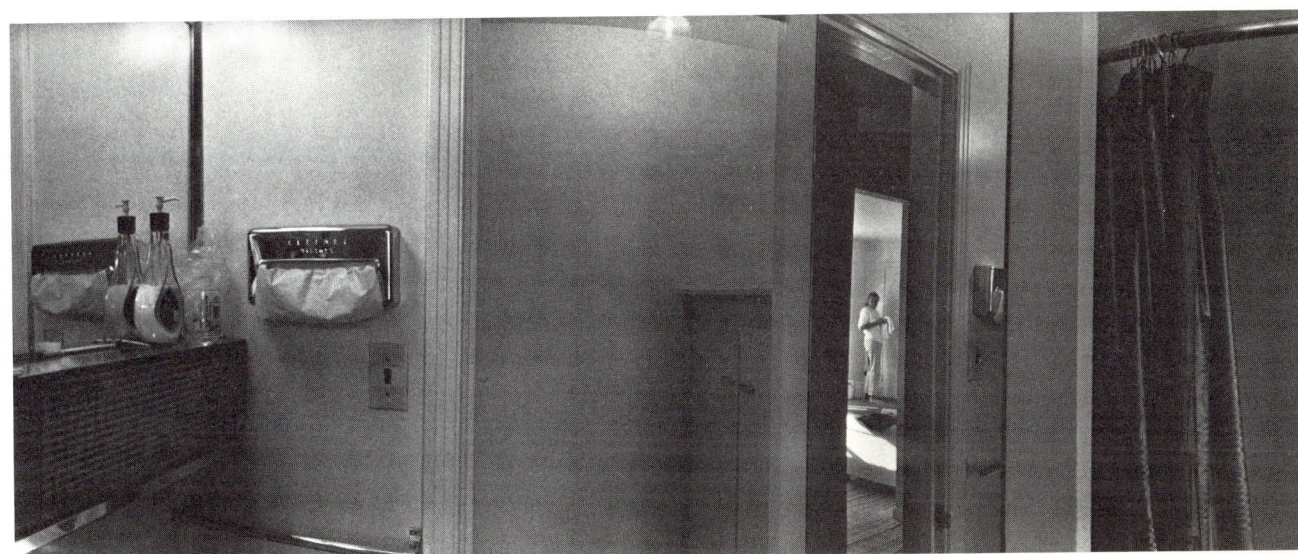

37 Anne Noggle, *Pismo Beach*, 1971

38 David Avison, *Central Park, New York City*, 1977

39 Oscar Bailey, *Backyard Event No. 2*, 1975

40 Jaroslav Poncar, *On the Siachen Glacier, East Karakorum, Pakistan*, 1978

41 Nina Schlosberg, *Wavy Line*, 1979.

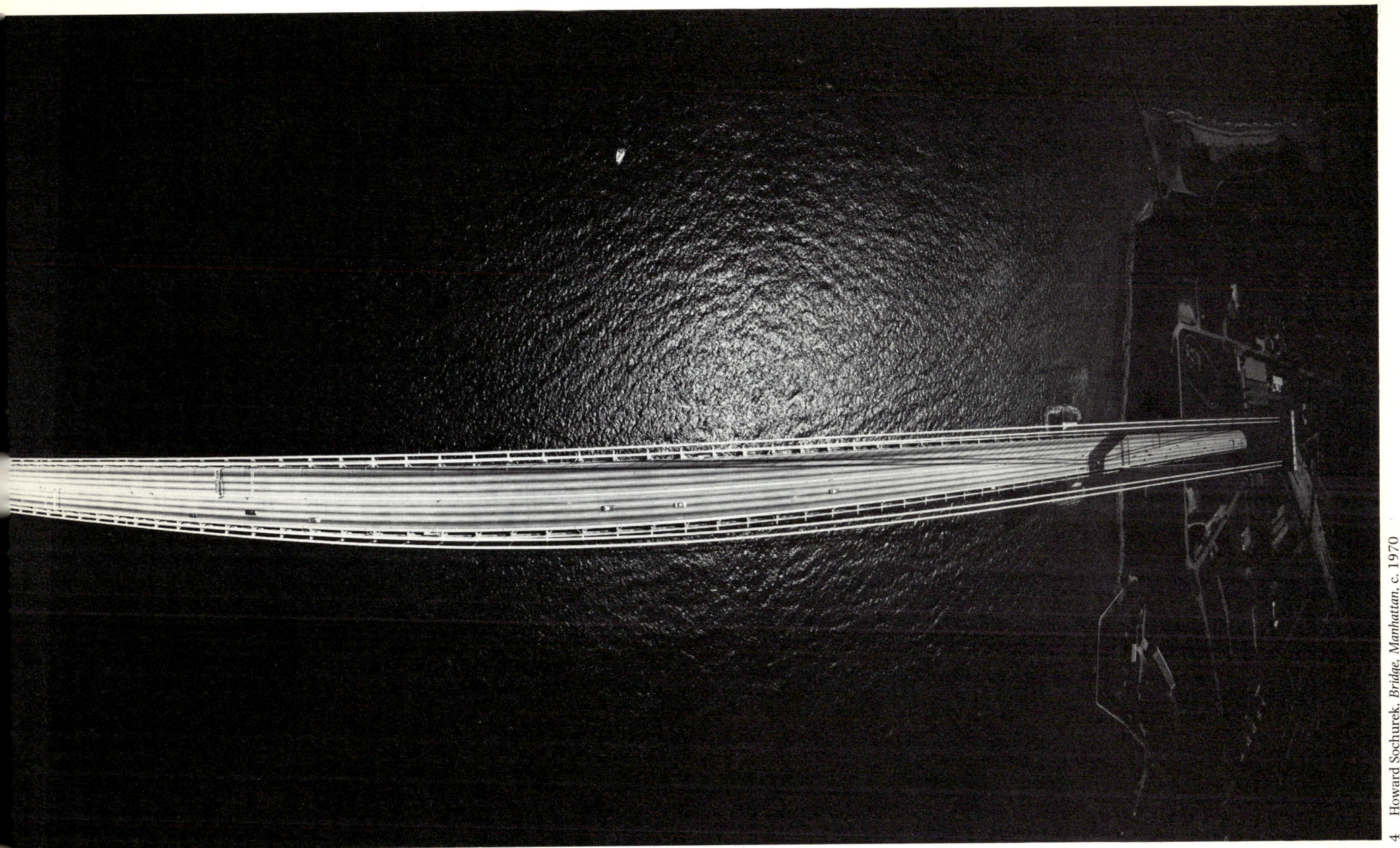

4 Howard Sochurek, *Bridge, Manhattan,* c. 1970

45

Catalogue

THE PANORAMIC IMAGE
THE PERIOD TO 1850

1. Albrecht DURER, (1471–1528)
   Siege of a Fortress, 1527
   Woodcut (two blocks), 21.9 cm × 72.1 cm, Bartsch 137,
   Campbell Dodgson 156.
   This print was probably intended for Dürer's *Befestigungswesen*,
   his treatise on fortification of 1527. Wealth of documentation
   and characteristic touches of fantasy make it, however, a
   remarkable early 'long view' in its own right.
   The British Museum.

2. Wenceslaus HOLLAR (1607–77)
   Three Views of Tangier, 1669
   (a) *from Peterborough Tower*. Pen and brown ink with
       watercolour, on nine sheets, 29.2 cm × 103.8 cm. Binyon
       34(b), Croft-Murray 31
   (b) *from the Land (South-west)*. Pen and brown ink with grey
       wash and watercolour, on three sheets, 32.4 cm × 90.8 cm,
       Binyon 33(b), Croft-Murray 28.
   (c) *from the Sea (North)*. Pen and brown ink with grey wash and
       watercolour on three sheets, 21.3 cm × 89.7 cm, Binyon
       33(a), Croft-Murray 35.
   Hollar made at least 23 drawings of Tangier, and in 1673
   published 12 etchings related to some of them together with
   three long prospects and a map. The present examples amply
   illustrate his mastery in composing for the long format.
   The British Museum.

3. Wenceslaus HOLLAR
   London from Southwark before and after the Great Fire, 1666.
   Etching (two plates), 22.5 cm × 68 cm, Parthey 1015
   The tower of St. Mary Overy (Southwark Cathedral) was the
   chief vantage point in the seventeenth century for views of
   London.
   The British Museum

4. Hendrick DANCKERTS (*c.* 1630–after 1679)
   Whitehall and Westminster from St. James's Park, c. 1675
   Pen and brown ink with watercolour, on three sheets,
   26.3 cm × 104.8 cm.
   Danckerts was from Holland, where artists became well
   practised in handling distant views. Here long, earth-hugging
   lines lead to the classical Banqueting House in the centre,
   steeper perspectives of pairs of trees to the Gothic Westminster
   Abbey on the right.
   The British Museum.

5. Francis PLACE (1647–1728)
   York from St. George's Close
   Pen and wash, on two sheets, 17.5 cm × 74.9 cm
   Place was a student of Hollar's views and those of the
   Dutchmen also.
   The British Museum.

6. ANON. GERMAN, late 18th century
   View from Mainz
   Pen and ink with grey wash, on three sheets, 34.9 cm × 107 cm
   A dramatic contrast is made, by means of a cluster of abrupt
   foreground verticals, between a tightly-planned garden and a
   wide-open riverscape—in a period strongly conscious of the
   contrast.
   The British Museum.

7. James BASIRE (1730–1802)
   The Encampment of the English Forces at Portsmouth in 1545,
   1778
   Line-engraving and etching, print area, 48.2 cm × 177.8 cm.
   The engraving, made from two plates, was after a drawing, now
   untraceable but perhaps by Charles Sherwin, from a sixteenth-
   century wall-painting at Cowdray Castle, Sussex, destroyed by
   fire in 1793. Basire prepared a series of such panorama-sized
   prints for the Society of Antiquaries. See the Society's *Vetusta
   Monumenta*, vol. 3, 1796.
   University of Southampton, Department of History

8. Thomas LONGCROFT (fl. 1786–93)
   Benares from the Ganges
   Pen and ink with grey wash on pale blue-grey paper,
   28.2 cm × 88.2 cm.
   A good example of the use of architecture with silhouette
   quality, so congenial to panoramists. The role of Islamic
   architecture—and the minaret in particular—was considerable
   here.
   The British Museum.

9. Henry Aston BARKER (1774–1856)
   Panorama of Paris, 1802
   Eight drawings, pencil and ink, each 35.6 cm × 53.3 cm.
   Made in May 1802 (during the brief peace in the French Wars)
   for the Paris panorama shown by Barker at Leicester Square in
   the following year.
   Victoria and Albert Museum

10. Decimus BURTON (1800–81)
    The Colosseum, Regent's Park, 1823
    (a) Section. Pen and ink and watercolour, 42.5 cm × 41.9 cm.
    (b) Plan. Pen and ink and watercolour, 32.4 cm × 31.1 cm.
    The site was south-east of the new Regent's Park, between
    Albany Street and Cambridge Terrace: the Royal College of
    Physicians now occupies it. The dome was 142 ft. across (30 ft.
    wider than St. Paul's) and rose 112 ft. from the ground. This
    very considerable building by a young architect of twenty-three
    was demolished by 1875, within his lifetime.
    Victorian and Albert Museum

11. Rudolph ACKERMANN (1764–1834), publisher
    Two of the *Graphic Illustrations of the Colosseum, Regent's Park*,
    five lithographs, 1829.
    (a) Plate III: Bird's eye view of London from a Painter's
        Platform, print area 28.1 cm × 21.1 cm.
    (b) Plate IV: Geometrical Ascent to the Galleries, print area
        28.1cm × 21.1cm.
    The 'geometrical ascent' was formed by a stairway enclosing an
    ascending platform. E. T. Parris and assistants are seen putting
    final touches to the painting. The covered area below was to be
    a 'salon' for showing works of art. See page 14.
    Guildhall Library, London

12. Thomas HORNOR (1785–1844)
    Plan of the Parish of Clerkenwell, London, 1813
    Aquatint, hand-coloured, print area, 58.4 cm × 90.2 cm.
    An example of the 'picturalised' map-making process followed
    by Hornor: the inclusion of cloud-shadow is particularly
    interesting. Such ideas were to lead him directly to panorama
    painting.
    Guildhall Library, London

13. Louis Jules ARNOUT (1814–68)
    'Greenwich en Ballon', from *Excursions Aériennes*, Paris, *c.* 1855.
    Lithograph, hand-coloured, 27.9 cm × 43.2 cm.
    Balloon journeys between Vauxhall Gardens, London, and
    continental locations such as Paris, or the duchy of Nassau,
    were popular from the 1820s, and public panoramas sometimes
    reproduced them.
    Guildhall Library, London

14. Robert HAVELL, Jr. (fl. 1820–50)
    South Kent (Costa scena—Cruise along the Southern Coast of Kent),
    1823
    Aquatint, hand-coloured, on cylinder, 10.1 cm × 355.6 cm.
    J. R. Abbey, *Life in England in Aquatint and Lithography
    1770–1860*, 1953, p. 383, no. 490, lists a version extending to
    Calais and a length of 576.2 cm.
    Victoria and Albert Museum

15. Robert HAVELL, Jr.
    London, 1822
    Aquatint, hand-coloured, on cylinder, 8.2 cm × 442 cm.
    See J. R. Abbey, op. cit. p. 382, No. 485.
    Victoria and Albert Museum

16. Thomas Mann BAYNES (1794–1854)

Two plates from *The North Bank of the Thames from Westminster Bridge to London Bridge*, 1825
Lithographs, hand-coloured, each, 26.6 cm × 66 cm.
This series of ten prints, together with map and prospectus, illustrated proposals by Lt.-Col. Trench (later General Sir Frederick Trench) for a quay and other improvements along the river.
Victoria and Albert Museum

17. Thomas SHEW (fl. 1825)
Rome 1825 (engraved by Thomas Sutherland)
Aquatint, 28.5 cm × 341.6 cm.
'Nothing is so beautiful as the lines of the Roman horizon . . .' wrote Chateaubriand in 1804 (*Voyage en Italie*), 'the valleys often assume the form of an arena, a circus or a hippodrome'. Shew was a member of the Academy of St. Luke at Rome.
Victoria and Albert Museum

18. Gottfried ENGELMANN (1788–1839)
Paris, c. 1825
Lithograph, hand-coloured, 10.1 cm × 330.2 cm.
The use of panorama format to illustrate street pastimes, processions and other incidents was popular in the 1820s.
Victoria and Albert Museum

19. David ROBERTS, R.A. (1796–1864)
Panoramic View of Cairo, 1839
Pencil and watercolour, 52.2 cm × 300.4 cm.
Robert Burford paid Roberts £50 for the copyright of this, using it for the panorama shown at Leicester Square in 1847 and engraved in the *Illustrated London News* of 20th March of that year.
Courtesy Fine Art Society, London

20. Sir George SCHARF (1820–95)
The Bavarian Alps from the Edge of Munich, 1846
Watercolour (two sheets), 18.4 cm × 71.1 cm, 19.3 cm × 35.9 cm.
Mont Blanc was first climbed in 1786, the same year that Robert Barker carried out the first full-circle panorama. The European Alps became a favourite subject for panoramists, both in themselves and, as here, as a distant presence within range of a famous city.
The British Museum

21. Handbill for the Eidophusikon, 'View in the Mediterranean by Moonlight, in the course of which will be introduced a Total Eclipse of the Moon'. 25.4 cm × 20.3 cm.
Datable 1780. Loutherbourg's show opened at his house in Lisle Street, London, in February 1781.
Guildhall Library, London

22. Brochure for panorama by Robert Barker, 'Lord Nelson's Defeat

of the French at the Nile', Leicester Square, 1799.
41.9 cm × 33.6 cm.
Guildhall Library, London

23. Brochure for 'Paris' panorama by Henry Aston Barker, Leicester Square, 1803. 28.7 cm × 22 cm.
David Robinson, Esq

24. Booklet, *Explanation . . . of the City of Paris*, Barker's Panorama, Strand, 1815. 20.6 cm × 13.1 cm.
David Robinson, Esq

25. 'Panorama of London, or a Day's Journey round the Metropolis. An Amusing and Instructive Game'.
Etching, hand-coloured, 53.3 cm × 54.6 cm.
Circa 1800.
Guildhall Library, London

26. Instructions for 'Panorama of London' game.
Jonathan Gestetner, Esq

27. Prospectus, *View of London and the surrounding country taken . . . from an Observatory purposely erected over the Cross of St. Paul's Cathedral*, by Thomas Hornor, 1822.
24.7 cm × 15.2 cm, opening to 95.2 cm × 90.2 cm.
Guildhall Library, London

28. Booklet, *A Description of the Colosseum, as reopened in MDCCCXLV*. 19.6 cm × 23.7 cm.
Datable 1851.
David Robinson, Esq

29. Leaflet, 'A Traveller in Spite of Yourself' (no date)
22.8 cm × 14.3 cm.
Guildhall Library, London.

30. Handbill, 'Stanfield's Grand Local Diorama', Theatre Royal, Drury Lane, 1824.
Guildhall Library, London

31. Brochure, 'The Funeral Procession of the Late Duke of York'.
Wood engraving, 20.3 cm × 54 cm.
The funeral of Frederick, Duke of York and Albany, took place from St. James's Palace on 20th January, 1827.
David Robinson Esq

32. Panorama of London in 1842, from the Duke of York's Column.
Wood-engravings made from daguerrotypes, total size 127 cm × 91.5 cm.
Illustrated London News, 7th January, 1843.
David Robinson Esq

THE PANORAMIC IMAGE 1850 TO THE PRESENT DAY

33. Bob CHAPLIN
High Tide, Low Tide, Eastern Isles, Scilly, 1979
Colour photographs, 55.9 cm × 83.8 cm
Collection Artist

34. Bob CHAPLIN
Low Tide, High Tide, Eastern Isles, Scilly, 1979
Colour photographs, 55.9 cm × 83.8 cm
Collection Artist

35. Bob CHAPLIN
Sunday Morning/Sunday Evening, Lingaholm, Orkney, 1979
Colour photographs, 55.9 cm × 83.8 cm
Collection Artist

36. Jan DIBBETS
A Circle and a Line, 1976–77
Photographs, pencil, paper, 75 cm × 100 cm
Collection Agnes & Frits Becht, Naarden, Holland

37. Rackstraw DOWNES
The Dam at Fairfield, 1974
Oil on canvas, 31.8 cm × 116.8 cm
Private Collection

38. Rackstraw DOWNES
The Softball Game, Skowhegan, 1975
Oil on canvas, 34.9 cm × 103.1 cm
Collection Beth Goldberg

39. Hamish FULTON
A 100-Mile Walk, 1975
Black and white photograph with text, 97.5 cm × 274.3 cm
Collection Arts Council of Great Britain

40. Vaughan GRYLLS
The Wailing Wall, Jerusalem, 1979
Photographs, 182.9 cm × 487.7 cm
Collection Artist

41. John HILLIARD
Ten Runs past a Fixed Point, 1971
Photographs, 78.7 cm × 48.3 cm
Collection Arts Council of Great Britain

42. Ivon HITCHENS
Giant Oak Tree and Open Sky, 1978
Oil on canvas, 44.5 cm × 109.2 cm
Collection Waddington Galleries Ltd

43. John LOKER
Vertical Extracts, 1977/8
Acrylic on canvas, 244 cm × 180 cm
Collection Artist

44. Richard LONG
A 2½ Day Circular Walk in the Scottish Highlands, 1979
Signwritten text, 243.8 cm × 243.8 cm
Collection Artist

45. Ed RUSCHA
Every Building on Sunset Strip, 1966
Fold-out book, 823 cm long
Published by Multiples Inc., N.Y.

46. Ed RUSCHA
Let's Keep in Touch, 1978
Silk screen print, 48.6 cm × 127.3 cm
Collection Multiples Inc., N.Y.

47. Ed RUSCHA
I've Never Seen Two People Looking Healthier, 1978
Silk screen print, 48.6 cm × 127.3 cm
Collection Multiples Inc., N.Y.

48. Susan SHATTER
Westhampton Beach, 1969
Watercolour on paper, 30.5 cm × 136 cm
Collection Artist

49. Susan SHATTER
Wigglesworth Fields, Ipswich, 1971
Watercolour on paper, 22.9 cm × 61 cm
Collection Artist

THE PANORAMIC IMAGE IN PHOTOGRAPHY

50. David AVISON
Central Park, New York City, 1977
Silver print, 26 cm × 81 cm
Collection Photographer

51. David AVISON
Near the Confluence of the Colorado and Green Rivers, Utah, 1972
Silver print, 26 cm × 81 cm
Collection Photographer

52. David AVISON
Smelt Fishing, Navy Pier, Chicago, 1975
Silver print, 26 cm × 81 cm
Collection Photographer

53. Oscar BAILEY
Backyard Event No. 2, 1975
Silver print, 21 cm × 121.6 cm
Collection Photographer

54. Oscar BAILEY
Cape May, New Jersey, 1977
Silver print, 18 cm × 122.2 cm
Collection Photographer

55. Oscar BAILEY
Minerva Spring, Yellowstone, 1975
Silver print, 22 cm × 111.3 cm
Collection Photographer

56. F. J. BANDHOLTS
Albia, Iowa, 1907
Silver print, 24.2 cm × 120.1 cm
Collection Library of Congress, Washington, D.C.

57. H. BARREUTHER
Northfield, Massachusetts, 1914
Silver print, 16.2 cm × 94.6 cm
Collection Library of Congress, Washington, D.C.

58. H. M. BEACH
From Black Bear Mountain, New York, 1911
Silver print, 15.3 cm × 111.5 cm
Collection Library of Congress, Washington, D.C.

59. Felice BEATO
Lucknow from the Kaiserbagh (from View of India after the Mutiny), 1857
Albumen print, 24.8 cm × 200.6 cm
Collection Victoria and Albert Museum, London

60. Kurt BENNING
London, 1980
Silver print, 13.5 cm × 125 cm
Collection Photographer

61. Adolphe BRAUN
'88 Panorama de Legg . . . horn, 1888
Carbon print, 20.4 cm × 45.7 cm
Collection Sam Wagstaff, New York

62. C. F. BRETZMAN
20th Annual Convention UMW of A, Indianapolis, Indiana, 1909
Silver print, 25.4 cm × 140.9 cm
Collection Library of Congress, Washington, D.C.

63. CALIFORNIA PANORAMA COMPANY
Four Irrigation Canals, Mesa, Arizona, 1908
Silver print, 23.3 cm × 179 cm
Collection Library of Congress, Washington, D.C.

64. A. CARPE
Mt. Fairweather, Alaska, n.d.
Silver prints, 7 parts on graph paper, 21.2 cm × 47 cm
Collection The National Archives, Washington, D.C.

65. Ralph CLEMENTS
Photograph of U.S.S. Los Angeles (Z–R–3) entering Hangar for the First Time at Lakehurst, New Jersey, c. 1925
Silver print, 18 cm × 108.6 cm
Collection Naval Historical Center, Navy Department, Washington, D.C.

66. Rusty CULP
Holiday Camp Homes
Silver print, 17.7 cm × 43.6 cm
Collection Photographer

67. Rusty CULP
Stripes and Planes, Paradise Park, Pharr, Texas, 1978
Silver print, 18 cm × 43.3 cm
Collection Photographer

68. George DAVISON
Mole Bridge, 1900
Gold-toned printing-out-paper, Kodak No. 1 Panoram,
5.6 cm × 17.4 cm
Collection The Kodak Museum, Harrow

69. George DAVISON
Untitled, view of Lowestoft, c. 1900
Gold-toned printing-out-paper, Kodak No. 4 Panoram,
8.2 cm × 29 cm
Collection The Kodak Museum, Harrow

70. George DAVISON
Untitled, view of Lowestoft, c. 1900
Gold-toned printing-out-paper, Kodak No. 4 Panoram,
7.8 cm × 29.5 cm
Collection The Kodak Museum, Harrow

71. George DAVISON
Untitled, view of shore, c. 1900
Gold-toned printing-out-paper, Kodak No. 1 Panoram,
5.5 cm × 17.1 cm
Collection The Kodak Museum, Harrow

72. Raymond DEPARDON
Sunset over Ghardaia, Algeria, 1969
Colour print, width 61 cm
Collection Raymond Depardon/Magnum Photos, Courtesy The

John Hillelson Agency, London

73. DETROIT PUBLISHING COMPANY
Skyline from Lakefront, Chicago, Illinois, n.d.
Silver print, 17.8 cm × 129.8 cm
Collection Library of Congress, Washington, D.C.

74. DICE & McCLYMONDS
Salute to 'La Marseillaise', Bastile Day, by 40,000 Camp Grant Soldiers, July 14, 1918
Silver print, 21 cm × 129 cm
Collection The National Archives, Washington, D.C.

75. FALK PHOTO COMPANY
Manhattan Beach, New York, 1902
Silver print, 25.1 cm × 79 cm
Collection Library of Congress, Washington, D.C.

76. E. R. FREEMAN
The California Redwoods, n.d.
Silver print, 18.9 cm × 118.8 cm
Collection International Museum of Photography at George Eastman House, Rochester, New York

77. E. O. GOLDBECK
Third Annual Bathing Girl Revue, Galveston, Texas, May 14, 1922
Silver print, 24.4 cm × 70.1 cm
Collection The Humanities Research Center, University of Texas at Austin

78. Fred S. GRAHAM
Whitestone Battlefield, North Dakota, 1914
Silver print, 18.5 cm × 115.5 cm
Collection Library of Congress, Washington, D.C.

79. THE HAINES PHOTO COMPANY
American Thread Company, Holyoke, Massachusetts, c. 1909
Silver print, 25 cm × 93 cm
Collection Library of Congress, Washington, D.C.

80. THE HAINES PHOTO COMPANY
The Parthenon, Nashville, Tennessee, January 16, 1909
Silver print, 25.5 cm × 97 cm
Collection Library of Congress, Washington, D.C.

81. THE HAINES PHOTO COMPANY
Seven Pines Battlefield, Virginia, 1912
Silver print, 25.1 cm × 76.8 cm
Collection Library of Congress, Washington, D.C.

82. D. W. HALL
CHSH IAN Ranch, California, 1913
Silver print, 23.4 cm × 109 cm

Collection Library of Congress, Washington, D.C.

83. HUDDLESTON PHOTO COMPANY
Oatman, Arizona, 1915
Silver print, 22.8 cm × 160 cm
Special Collections, the University of Arizona Library, Tucson

84. HUGHES PHOTOGRAPHIC COMPANY
Western Maryland Dairy, n.d.
Silver print, 25.1 cm × 135.3 cm
Edward L. Bafford Collection, University of Maryland, Baltimore County, U.S.A.

85. Gerald INCANDELA
Old New York, 1978
Silver print, 50.8 cm × 61 cm
Collection Photographer

86. Rev. Calvert JONES
45. Bay of Baid and 46. Baid, 1845/6
Calotypes, two prints marked for joining into panorama, each 18.5 cm × 22.6 cm
Collection Science Museum, Fox Talbot Collection, London

87. W. H. JONES
Hyde Park and Westport High School, Kansas City, Missouri, 1909
Silver print, 25 cm × 121 cm
Collection Library of Congress, Washington, D.C.

88. W. H. JONES
Swope Park, Kansas City, Missouri, 1909
Silver print, 25 cm × 121 cm
Collection Library of Congress, Washington, D.C.

89. Michel Szulz KRZYZANOWSKI
Andros 8, January 1977
Silver prints, 9 parts, 70 cm × 100 cm
Collection Photographer

90. George R. LAWRENCE
International Ballooning Contest, Aero park, Chicago, Illinois, July 4, 1908
Silver print, 43.5 cm × 116 cm
Collection Library of Congress, Washington, D.C.

91. George R. LAWRENCE
San Francisco in Ruins from Lawrence Captive Airship 2000 feet above San Francisco Bay Overlooking Waterfront, 1906
Silver print, 47.6 cm × 123.8 cm
Collection Library of Congress, Washington, D.C.

92. George R. LAWRENCE
Untitled, Beer Garden filled with customers, n.d.

Silver print, 59 cm × 99 cm
Collection Library of Congress, Washington, D.C.

93. George R. LAWRENCE
San Francisco Two Years After, Photograph from the Lawrence Captive Airship, 1908
Photogravure, 32.5 cm × 81 cm
Collection Jonathan Bayer

94. C. L. McCLURE
Buena Vista and Collegiate Range, Colorado, 1911
Gold-toned, 18.4 cm × 107.9 cm
Collection Library of Congress, Washington, D.C.

95. MOFFETT STUDIO
Leaning Tower, Baptistry and Cathedral, Pisa, Italy, 1909
Silver print, 25 cm × 103.5 cm
Collection Library of Congress, Washington, D.C.

96. R. MOORE
Gannets, Cape Kidnappers, New Zealand, c. 1910
Hand coloured, 24 cm × 89 cm
Collection Sam Wagstaff, New York

97. Eadweard MUYBRIDGE
Panorama of San Francisco from California Street Hill, 1877
Silver prints, 13 parts, 55.5 cm × 526.5 cm
Collection Central Library, Museum and Art Gallery, Royal Borough of Kingston-upon-Thames

98. ALMERON NEWMAN PHOTO COMPANY
Camp Cody, New Mexico, June 1918
Silver print, 18.4 cm × 292 cm
Special Collections, the University of Arizona Library, Tucson

99. Anne NOGGLE
La Posada, 1969
Silver print, approx. width 192 cm
Collection Photographer

100. Anne NOGGLE
Pismo Beach, 1971
Silver print, approx. width 192 cm
Collection Photographer

101. PHOTOGRAPHER UNIDENTIFIED
Coney Island, New York, 1921
Silver print, 25.1 cm × 107 cm
Collection Library of Congress, Washington, D.C.

102. PHOTOGRAPHER UNIDENTIFIED
Apollo 15 Landing Site
Silver prints, 2 parts, 21.9 cm × 45.7 cm

Collection World Data Center, Greenbelt, Maryland

103. PHOTOGRAPHER UNIDENTIFIED
Monte Carlo Album, c. 1910
Silver prints, 24 views, each 8.7 cm × 29.6 cm
Collection Science Museum, London

104. PHOTOGRAPHER UNIDENTIFIED
Untitled; Celebration at St. Cloud, France, n.d.
Silver print, Damoizeau Cyclograph, 17.1 cm × 56.7 cm
Collection International Museum of Photography at George
Eastman House, Rochester, New York

105. PHOTOGRAPHER UNIDENTIFIED
Untitled: causeway, c. 1901
Gold-toned printing-out-paper, Kodak No. 4 Panoram,
8.5 cm × 29.6 cm
Collection The Kodak Museum, Harrow

106. PHOTOGRAPHER UNIDENTIFIED
Untitled; boats on water, c. 1901
Gold-toned printing-out-paper, Kodak No. 1 Panoram,
5.3 cm × 17.3 cm
Collection The Kodak Museum, Harrow

107. PHOTOGRAPHER UNIDENTIFIED
Untitled; two men and car in desert, n.d.
Modern silver print from original negative, 20 cm × 212 cm
Collection Arizona Historical Society, Henry and Albert
Buehman Memorial Collection, Tucson

108. PHOTOGRAPHER UNIDENTIFIED
Untitled; 'Bellingham for Christ', n.d.
Silver print, 14.8 cm × 121.5 cm
Collection Library of Congress, Washington, D.C.

109. PHOTOGRAPHER UNIDENTIFIED
Paris, c. 1844
Daguerreotype, 8.9 cm ×.30.5 cm
Collection Science Museum, London

110. Jaroslav PONCAR
On the Siachen Glacier, East Karakorum, Pakistan, 1978
Silver print, 9 cm × 36.8 cm
Collection Photographer

111. Jaroslav PONCAR
Two Black Hills near Ridah, North Yemen, 1977
Silver print, 9 cm × 37 cm
Collection Photographer

112. Jaroslav PONCAR
Village Potoskar in Zanskar, 1976

Silver print, 9 cm × 35.9 cm
Collection Photographer

113. Victor Albert PROUT
Harleyford, c. 1865
Albumen print, 110 cm × 280 cm
Collection The Royal Photographic Society, Bath

114. Eric RENNER
Ice House, Ticul, Mexico, 1969
Silver print, Pinhole Camera, 23.9 cm × 72.4 cm
Collection Photographer

115. William RIDER-RIDER
Troops of the 3rd Canadian Division, Entering Cambrai, France,
9 October 1918.
Silver print, 9.9 cm × 34.1 cm
Collection Public Archives of Canada, National Photography
Collection

116. William RIDER-RIDER
Passchendaele (Belgium) now a Field of mud, November 1917
Silver print, 9.9 cm × 34.1 cm
Collection Public Archives of Canada, National Photography
Collection

117. Richard ROSS
Charlie Wax, St. Augustine, Florida, 1977
Gum bichromate, 25.7 cm × 67.3 cm
Collection Photographer

118. Richard ROSS
Sidney at Coney Island, New York, 1979
Gum bichromate, 20.2 cm × 80 cm
Collection Photographer

119. ROYAL PHOTO COMPANY
Untitled, July 4, 1915
Silver print, 22.4 cm × 183 cm
Collection Library of Congress, Washington, D.C.

120. Sherie SCHEER
Surfers, 1980
Silver print, painted with oils, 35.8 cm × 134.4 cm
Collection Photographer

121. Sherie SCHEER
270° Venice Beach, 1978/80
Silver print, painted with oils, 30.7 cm × 153.6 cm
Collection Photographer

122. Nina SCHLOSBERG
'79 Wavy Line, 1979

Silver print, 24.1 cm × 10.2 cm
Collection Photographer

123. Nina SCHLOSBERG
Room with Three Girls, 1978
Silver print, 21.5 cm × 9.1 cm
Collection Photographer

124. F. J. SCHLUETER
Goose Creek Oil Field, Texas, 1919
Silver print, 18.5 cm × 119 cm
Collection Library of Congress, Washington, D.C.

125. Kathryn SCHOOLEY-ROBINS
Crabber, Gwynn Island, Virginia, 1977
Hand-coloured cyanotype, 5.3 cm × 69 cm
Collection Photographer

126. Kathryn SCHOOLEY-ROBINS
San Xavier No. 2, 1977
Hand-coloured cyanotype, 5.5 cm × 45.4 cm
Collection Photographer

127. SCHUTZ
*General Pershing and Major General Dickman with the Officers and
Men of the 2nd Division, Valendar, Germany,* March 1919
Silver print, 19 cm × 94 cm
Collection Library of Congress, Washington, D.C.

128. SCHUTZ
*Lens, France, The Devastated Coal Mining Region of Northern
France, 220 Coal Pits Rendered Useless,* 1919
Silver print, 19.7 cm × 106.7 cm
Collection Library of Congress, Washington, D.C.

129. SCHUTZ
The Railway Station Plaza, Arras, France, February 1919.
Silver print, 20 cm × 106.3 cm
Collectin Library of Congress, Washington, D.C.

130. SHEELOR PHOTO
Miles and Childs Glacier, Alaska, 1915
Silver print, 24 cm × 145.9 cm
Collection Library of Congress, Washington, D.C.

131. Art SINSABAUGH
Chicago Landscape, No. 117, 1964
Silver print, 10.3 cm × 49.3 cm
Collection International Museum of Photography at George
Eastman House, Rochester, New York

132. Art SINSABAUGH
Midwest Landscape, No. 34, 1961

Silver print, 5.2 cm × 48.3 cm
Collection Sam Wagstaff, New York

133. Kenneth SNELSON
New Jersey Skyline, 1979
Contact print, 40.3 cm × 121.6 cm
Collection Photographer

134. Kenneth SNELSON
Paris—Women with Umbrella, 1975
Cibachrome print, 10.8 cm × 78.7 cm
Collection Photographer

135. Kenneth SNELSON
Sacre Coeur with Buses, 1975
Cibachrome print, 10.8 cm × 78.7 cm
Collection Photographer.

136. Kenneth SNELSON
Paris Alley with Two Arches, 1975
Cibachrome print, 10.8 cm × 78.7 cm
Collection Photographer

137. Howard SOCHUREK
HS3 Aerial of Bridge, New York City, 1970
Colour print, 30.5 cm × 61 cm
Collection Howard Sochurek, courtesy The John Hillelson
Agency, London

138. Howard SOCHUREK
HS6 Aerial of New York City, 1970
Colour print, 30 cm × 61 cm
Collection Howard Sochurek, courtesy The John Hillelson
Agency, London

139. J. W. STEPHENSON
Fort Rock, Oregon, 1911
Silver print, 16.2. cm × 115 cm
Collection Library of Congress, Washington, D.C.

140. Josef SUDEK
Prague
Silver print, 15.7 cm × 50.8 cm
Collection David Dawson Gallery Ltd., London

141. Josef SUDEK
The Enchanted Garden, c. 1956
Silver print, 92 cm × 286 cm
Collection Peter Turner, London

142. William Henry FOX TALBOT
Orleans, June 1843

Modern salt print from original negative, 15.9 cm × 52.3 cm
Collection The Kodak Museum, Harrow

143. UNDERWOOD AND UNDERWOOD
*Panorama View, Sheepshead Bay, Motor Board Track—Showing
Mammoth Grandstand*, 1915
Silver print, 18.6 cm × 108.6 cm
Collection Library of Congress, Washington, D.C.

144. Oleg H. VOLDENG and Eric BOLTON
Medicine Hat, Alberta, 1913
Silver print, 12.7 cm × 239.9 cm
Collection Public Archives of Canada, National Photography
Collection

145. Laura VOLKERDING
Chicago, 1978
Silver print, 26.4 cm × 56.8 cm
Collection Photographer

146. Laura VOLKERDING
Las Vegas, New Mexico, 1978
Silver print, 26.4 cm × 56.8 cm
Collection Photographer

147. Laura VOLKERDING
Sacramento Metropolitan KOA, 1978
Silver print, 26.4 cm × 56.8 cm
Collection Photographer

148. R. J. WATERS
The Burning City, San Francisco, 10 a.m. April 18, 1906
Silver print, 22.5 cm × 140 cm
Collection John Hillelson

149. R. J. WATERS
The Desolate City, 1906
Silver print, 24 cm × 145 cm
Collection John Hillelson

List of Illustrations